Co
Kno

John

COLLECTING NOW: KNOW YOUR PICTURE

JOHN FITZMAURICE MILLS

ARIEL BOOKS

BRITISH BROADCASTING CORPORATION

By the same author:
Collecting Now: Care and Repair of Your Antiques

Drawings by David Brown

Published by the
British Broadcasting Corporation
35 Marylebone High Street
London W1M 4AA

ISBN 0 563 20208 4 (paperback)
        0 563 20249 1 (hardback)

First published 1984
© John FitzMaurice Mills 1984

Typeset by Phoenix Photosetting, Chatham
Printed in Great Britain by Mackays of Chatham Ltd

This book is set in 10 on 11 point Ehrhardt Linotron

Contents

Acknowledgements
I would like to express my gratitude to those friends in the Conservation Laboratory, the National Gallery, London, and the Technical Department, the Courtauld Institute, London, who answered many questions. Further to the Director of the National Museum of Ireland, the Chester Beatty Library, Dublin, and the Sheffield Municipal Galleries. My grateful thanks also to Dr A. E. Werner for reading through the manuscript of this book, as he did also with my book *Treasure Keepers*, published in 1973, and with *The Practice & History of Painting* my first book on the subject, published in 1959. Finally a word of gratitude to Sheila Elkin of BBC Publications.

John FitzMaurice Mills

Cavemen to Egyptians, Early Greeks and Romans

The arts of painting and drawing cannot be said, if one looks at the practical reality, to be essential to the existence of the human race. Yet to those who trace the development of these arts through history it would appear that they have been needed to satisfy the aesthetic and possibly subconscious cravings of man for a very long time indeed. The first traces of picture-making date back to around 20,000 BC.

In caves at places like Altamira in Spain and Lascaux in France paintings have been discovered that have a wonderful vitality. On the ceilings and walls of rock the painted animals have, in some cases, a sense of active movement that was not bettered until the camera showed artists the action of animals' bodies and legs when galloping and leaping. More primitive evidence of later man's efforts at artistic expression have been brought to light in other parts of the world; South Africa with the work of the Bushmen, rock engravings in Scandinavia and Mount Pellegrino, Palermo in Sicily and comparatively recent examples by such as the aboriginals of Western Arnhem Land, North Australia.

The fascinating point which has still not been totally understood is just why these peoples should have painted and drawn as they did. Our earliest ancestors seem to have arrived and to have been walking around on two legs some half a million years ago, yet there is an enormous time-gap during which very little is known as to just what they did with their hands, other than simple artefacts chipped from stones that have survived. Then, during the final stages of the Paleolithic, or Old Stone Age, the cave paintings appear.

Early man must have suddenly felt a need to communicate, to pass on ideas. It has been suggested that because he showed the beasts he had to hunt for his food he may have been trying to cast spells upon them, as a number are depicted with spears and some sort of arrows sticking in them. Was he attempting to record his achievements or may he have just been painting and drawing for the joy in the accomplishment? His palette of colours was very limited: ochres that could range in tint from yellow to red, iron oxides occurring in haematite and limonite which could produce dark browns and manganese dioxide for black; possibly, charcoal or charred sticks were used, although the dark greys and blacks from these sources would not have had the permanence of the manganese dioxide except under some special conditions for their preservation. Depending on the area, other oxides or earth colours may have been available, ranging from the warmth of sienna to the powerful deep tones of the umbers. It is interesting to note that these earth colours have remained the permanent backbone of the painter's palette throughout history, colours such as yellow ochre, raw sienna and raw umber are reliable pigments whether with water colour, tempera or oil today.

It is apparent that these early artists had discovered the need to reduce the pigments where possible to powders, perhaps pounding them with stones or grinding them between two flat stones. In some cases it is likely that they used the colours in sticks roughly sharpened to the shape of primitive pastels. Exactly which substances were used as vehicles for the powdered pigments is not certain; suggestions include animal fat, blood, bone marrow, honey, milk and water. Owing to the long period of time since these paintings were carried out it is impossible to verify the actual substances used, although if the surface of the rock was damp it would seem to rule against fatty materials, which would not have adhered to the rock. Blood would have blackened; yet it may have been used if the pictures had some religious, magical or superstitious implication. As the rock surface was porous, it would, however, have accepted the colours just mixed with water. Numbers of simple dishes in which the paints were mixed have been found.

Apart from the sharpened lumps of pigment, the colours could have been applied with the thumb and fingers in the manner of finger painting – as is taught in junior schools today – quite thick paint being squeezed out from under a thumb to form a strong line or accent. Chewed sticks could have been used as simple brushes, even small pads of animal fur may have been employed to spread out areas of colour. Whether early man attempted to make actual paint brushes by attaching hairs or bristles to sticks with some form of glue or binding is not known. Another technique which was sometimes used was a form of spraying – either by means of a hollow bone or one that had been made into a channel shape – evidence of this appears at Lascaux. Whether drawing, painting or spraying, the often rough and irregular surface of the rock demanded a brave and sweeping style with simple forms. At Altamira it would seem that the painters exploited the texture of the rocks and obtained effects of considerable realism and action in some cases. From examples of cave art it is evident that the artists were conscious of the third dimension and tried to simulate it by an overlapping of forms. The large majority of subjects are of animals; when the human form is portrayed it is nearly always in profile, as a face front on would have presented the draughtsman with the problem of foreshortening. It is likely that the human figures that were included would be thought of as supernatural beings or sorcerers. At Les Trois-Frères is a man wearing antlers on his head and at Le Gabillou another with a pair of bison horns.

What early man had established was that a painting could become a form of international language, and that its content, or most of it, could communicate itself to almost anyone at any time and in any place.

The development of writing using letters and characters stems in a number of cases from the visual portrayals of the artist – witness the development of the hieroglyphic symbols of the ancient Egyptians and the Sumerian picture-signs which progress stage by stage into cuneiform. The Aztecs in Mexico had an advanced form of pictographic writing which, after a little study, is still comprehensible. Today we are surrounded by ideograms, visual signs which stand for ideas or objects and which are not tied to a specific language; these may be representational or symbolic, such as traffic signs, or the realist pictorial abbreviations to be found, for instance, in guide-books.

The visual arts of painting and drawing are born out of a need to communicate, and from this point a long journey towards perfection of accomplishment begins. This struggle still goes on. Painting and drawing are crafts as well as arts, what is more they are difficult crafts. Watching the hand of a master using a brush or pastel can make the creation of a picture look quite simple. But skill achieved over years of practice can be deceptive. The performance succeeds because a great mass of knowledge has been absorbed: how a subject should be portrayed, how the brush or pastel will perform, how the colours will mix with the different media, how the oils, gums and emulsions will react, how to prepare the panel, paper or canvas. To all these is added a comprehension of composition, form relationship, perspective and the almost infinite subtleties of light, reflected light, half-tones and full shadow, and the appreciation for the artist grows. As prowess increases, so the individual starts to express something that it is more difficult to pinpoint. The truly great artist puts down a visual image of his personal ideas, translations of an emotive force released from a mind that will have culled inspiration from mental or physical experience. The pictures we hang on our walls are all a part of this process, whether large oil paintings, gentle water colours, delicate pencil drawings or prints; we choose them generally for the simple reason that we like them. There is something about each one that appeals irresistibly. It may be the subject matter, the treatment of the light, the use of colour – perhaps it is that, in some elusive way, an owner of a work of art feels akin with the original artist and thus the warmth of the initial inspiration is reflected from the picture.

To know something about the manner in which different paintings and drawings have been worked is to enjoy them more. The techniques of the artist have well-nigh endless variations, his tools are often personal, the materials painted and drawn on are numerous, and when it comes to the pigments, the colours and the oils, varnishes, liquids, and strange additives he uses, the whole process of preparing things can make parts of the studio seem like a kitchen. Ancient manuscripts detail recipes for cooking up colours and mediums that can have some revolting ingredients – and also be at times highly lethal for the poor unfortunate apprentice or studio assistant.

One of the earliest inventions for the artist was the basic convention of a draughtsmanship with which he could delineate a subject by enclosing it with lines to make it recognisable. To this image could then be added colour. The story of the progress of picture-making would appear to have stagnated for thousands of years after the cavemen and it is not until the early Egyptians that the arts and crafts really received a noticeable impetus. The Pharaohs and their priests saw in painting and sculpture a means to carry a propaganda message to the world they imagined lay on the other side of the veil. Thus the Pharaohs and priests constructed with the Pyramids, temples and rock tombs, some of the most amazing architectural works of any time. Thousands of slaves must have burnt out their poor lives to bring into being these great monuments, many of which remain to convey to us, in the 20th century, the strength and atmosphere they originally possessed. Wall decoration was in low relief carving, left plain or sometimes coloured, or in painted murals. In the heart of the

the tombs could often be found the finest of the work. The painters and craftsmen, and the priests, were probably the only people who would have seen the finished work.

When the painting of the early Egyptians is examined, one becomes conscious of a strange method of delineation of some areas which is particularly noticeable with figures. The heads are shown in profile, but the eyes are drawn in as though full face, and this rather odd distortion is carried on down the body; the shoulders are full towards the viewer, the hips and legs are in profile, whilst the feet are generally shown in profile from the inside – so that the figure can appear to have two right or two left feet. One of the underlying reasons behind this strange configuration is that the dictate for the artist was to make everything clear, instantly recognisable to a code of representation. The paintings were intended to be a commentary, very nearly a form of journalistic reporting on the particular Pharaoh or top person; an account for those he was to meet in his afterlife. Scale is used to clarify the important persons: so the Pharaoh may stand ten times taller than the mass of servants surrounding him. The profile convention was also extended to the painting of animals, birds and fish, all of which are shown with considerable accuracy.

The principal supports for painting were stone, plaster, rough canvas-like textiles, papyrus, wood and pottery. The earliest known example of mural painting is of predynastic date and is carried out on a form of clay plaster. Later a more refined method called for a gypsum plaster to which might be added a type of water-soluble glue, thus making an early form of *gesso*. The stone could be alabaster, quartzite, schist, granite, sandstone or limestone; with the last two being in preponderance. The normal practice before painting the walls of tombs and temples was to apply a thin coat of whitewash. The canvas could be given a grounding of tinted opaque wash, probably with some form of aqueous binder; wood also would have a priming which might be a thin layer of the gesso mentioned above.

The palette of colours available for the Egyptian artist was considerably in advance of the caveman's and it allowed for rich and cheerful effects. First and foremost he had blue pigments, one was carbonate of copper that is found in the eastern desert and Sinai; this substance is known as azurite. But the more favoured blue for the early Egyptian painter was an artificial frit that was made by heating together silica, a copper compound (which could have often been malachite), calcium carbonate and natron. There are a number of accounts of this rather lovely colour, including one written around 40 BC by Vitruvius. Vitruvius was a Roman architect, who wrote *De Architectura*, the only classical work on architecture which has survived. He states that the Egyptian blue frit was invented in Alexandria and he calls it *coeruleum*, a name still used by some colourmen for the pale limpid blue also known as cerulean; actually his facts are incorrect, because the frit was known of at least two thousand years before Alexandria was built. Various chemists have since investigated its properties, among them Sir Humphry Davy of safety lamp fame and W. J. Russell, who succeeded in reproducing samples of the pigment.

The black used was a form of carbon, this could have been soot scraped from kitchen utensils which could give a strong tone. Sometimes evidence has been found that a weaker black was made from a mixture of powdered charcoal and a wax, probably from bees; manganese black has also been identified, this material can be found quite plentifully in Sinai. A pleasant green colour could have been made from ground up malachite. Two yellows were known: yellow ochre, an earth colour found locally which takes its tint from hydrated oxide of iron, and a naturally occurring sulphide of arsenic, this was known as orpiment. In its natural state orpiment is not poisonous, but if, however, it is manufactured in fairly large quantities, as it was much later in Europe, it is very poisonous, and in the end its use had to be discontinued.

Reds were either red iron oxide or red ochres, and orange was normally obtained by mixing one of these with a yellow or over-painting a yellow with a red. Pink was a tint that appeared in a number of the tombs, notably those of the 18th Dynasty ruler Amenemhet and Nofretete of the 19th Dynasty. This was probably prepared from red ochre with gypsum and later, during the Graeco-Roman period, by the use of madder root. The whites could have been either calcium carbonate in the form of chalk or calcium sulphate as gypsum, another suggestion is that use may have been made of powdered shells or cuttle-fish bone. Their grey would have been a mixture of one of the whites with charcoal or with lamp black.

The distance of time has made it difficult to discover exactly what substances the Egyptians mixed with their pigments. But an examination of the paint films shows that the colours were not mixed with oils, and this points to the fact that the paint was some kind of tempera, an emulsion or glue-bound mixture. Glues available would have included gums from plants, also a

size, a gelatine that could have been obtained from animal products or fish bones; it is likely too that egg white was used, this
last would have given a strong resilient film. Another binder was
undoubtedly beeswax, which was used not only mixed with the
pigments but also as a protective coating afterwards. Moreover
they made use of a near colourless varnish to coat murals,
coffins, wooden canopic boxes and wooden stelae.

The palettes the painters used for holding and mixing their
colours were normally rectangular in shape with either a circular
or rectangular depression and were made from stone and in
some special cases from ivory – two palettes from this material
were found in the tomb of Tutankhamun – and gold-covered
wood – an example of which was discovered in the same tomb.
The paint brushes were primitive by today's skilfully made
examples. They were made from vegetable fibres, commonly
from the rib of the branches of the date palm. The strips would
be bruised to cause the individual fibres to separate, and the
resulting object would be something like a present-day shaving
brush, varying from two to three millimetres in diameter up to a
centimetre and a half. Some writers have also suggested that use
may have been made of various feathers, although this has not
been confirmed.

In the Fayum province of Egypt wooden panels for placing
over the faces of mummies came to light; on these were facial
likenesses presumably corresponding with those of the
mummified figures. The portraits date from the Roman period,
and are carried out in a wax technique. Their extraordinary lifelike appearance has lasted right through the centuries, in a
number of cases with little sign of the deterioration which might
be expected from more conventional media. The technique
clearly indicates the use of heat with the application of the
colours, but apart from that much of the practice of 'encaustic',
as this method is called, is hidden by time and argument. That
walking encyclopedia the Elder Pliny, who was writing during
the 1st century AD, left behind a relevant paragraph:

> In ancient times there were two methods of encaustic
> painting with wax on ivory with the cestrum, until it
> became the custom to paint ships of war. Then the third
> method was added, that of melting the wax colours, and
> laying them on with a brush. This kind of painting applied
> to ships is proof against sun, wind and salt water.

The wax Pliny was referring to would have quite clearly been beeswax. The ancients had no knowledge of sugar and used honey for sweetening, thus beeswax was in plentiful supply. But this wax by itself never sets really hard and certainly in a hot climate would retain a perpetual tackiness. So, to make it suitable for the painting technique which was used on the mummy boards, it would have to be hardened in some way. Thorough purification helped, but by itself was not sufficient. Pliny and Fioscurides both talk about melting the beeswax in sea-water and then mixing in some soda; this, apart from whitening the beeswax, also appeared to have hardened it. It is possible also that amounts of natural resin could have been combined with the wax. This is a method much used in picture restoration and the resulting substance has considerable adhesive powers and a good surface hardness with no tackiness.

But the arguments really come in connection with the application of the colours. Many art historians have tried to discover the full secrets of this remarkable technique, but few have met with any great measure of success. In 1760 a manual on encaustic was published by J. H. Muntz and printed privately for him by A. Webley, at the Bible and Crown near Chancery Lane, Holborn. This set out to describe a certain Count Caylus's 'Method of Painting in the Manner of the Ancients'. It begins by stating that Count Caylus, a member of the Academy of Inscriptions, had undertaken to explain an obscure passage in Pliny the naturalist and how there is talk that 'the ancients painted with burnt wax' and that such pictures were very durable. The passage in Pliny which is referred to is in Book XXXV chapter 11 and reads:

> Who first invented to paint with (or in) wax, and burn in (or fix) the picture with fire, is not certainly known. Some think Aristides invented it, and that Praxiteles brought it to perfection: but there were pictures by masters, of a much older date; such as Polignote, Nicanor and Arcefilaus, all artists of Paros.
>
> Lysippus writ upon his pictures he burnt in, which he would not have done if the encaustic had not been invented then.

The whole matter of early wax painting methods is complicated, not only by the different translations and readings of the old accounts, but also by the fact that there were a number of ways in which the manner was used. The name encaustic is derived from the Greek for 'burnt in'. It is generally applied to paintings which have wax as the principal vehicle and thus call for the application of heat at some stage of their execution. The permanence of beeswax and its power of resisting damp, mould growths and insect attack, as well as its adherence, were all well known to the Egyptians and the Greeks. The latter and the Romans used it for the protection of their sculptures. The process was termed *Ganosis* and an extract from Vitruvius gives some hint of the elaborate treatment:

> But anybody who is more particular and wants a polished finish of vermilion that will keep its proper colour, should, after the wall has been polished and is dry, apply with a brush punic wax, (this implies beeswax that has had some treatment or additives to render the cooled wax harder) melted over a fire and mixed with a little oil: then after this he should bring the wax to a sweat by warming it and the wall at close quarters with charcoal enclosed in an iron vessel; and finally he should smooth it all off by rubbing it down with a wax candle and clean linen cloths, just as naked marble statues are treated. This process is called *Ganosis* in Greek. The protecting coat of punic wax prevents the light of the moon and the rays of the sun from licking up and drawing the colour out of such polished finishing.

Ancient writers often mentioned encaustic, and earlier readings of the accounts confused it with a form of enamelling. But when Pliny and other scribes come up with terms such as '*incausto pingere*', '*pictura encaustica*', '*ceris pingere*' and '*pictura inurere*' it points to the fact that it is a painting method with its own techniques. Undoubtedly, the application of wax either with or to the colours, gave them a translucence and particular richness not achievable by other methods. The trouble was that the whole process tended to be extremely complicated and demanding on the painter. One of the stumbling blocks was, and still is, that the exact composition of the Punic wax is unknown. The chevalier Lorgna who researched the subject stated that the *nitron* mentioned by Pliny is not the nitre of the moderns, but the *natron* of the ancients, the native salt which can be found crystallised in Egypt and other hot countries in the sands surrounding lakes of salt water. Pliny states that this was the substance used by the Carthaginians when preparing their wax; from this was derived the name of Punic wax. Lorgna experimented along these lines, trying out various proportions of wax to salt. He heated the mixture in an iron vessel over a slow fire and stirred it with a wooden spoon, until the resulting mass resembled butter with the pale colour of milk. After it had been cooled it was found that it would liquefy in water and a milky emulsion was produced which could be made into a high-quality soap.

It is recorded that the 18th-century Italian painter Antonio Paccheri decorated the apartments of the Count Giovanni Battista Gasola using this wax vehicle plus a small amount of gum-arabic; after the work was finished he treated the surface with caustic and then rubbed the walls down with linen cloths, and the colours came up with a peculiar brightness and vivacity.

Count Caylus started his experiments by blending oil of turpentine with the beeswax and using this as a vehicle for the colours. This, however, does not explain Pliny's reference to 'burning', also it was found that the oil of turpentine made the waxy paste dry out too quickly, so that the painter did not have enough time to work his colours into the picture. The second attempt seems rather nearer to Pliny. With this, the wax was mixed with a strong solution of salt of tartar and into this mixture the colours were then ground. When the picture was finished, heat was applied gradually, and this apparently caused the wax to melt and swell and become bloated up upon the picture. If the heat were then slowly dropped, it would be found that the colours had in no way been injured by the heat, in fact they would have become unalterable – so much so that spirits of wine have been spilt upon them without causing the slightest harm.

The method that the Count finally evolved was somewhat more simple. First, the wooden support for the picture should be well rubbed over with a piece of beeswax. Secondly, the pigments should be mixed up with water. Then, as the colours so prepared would not adhere to the wax, the whole support should be rubbed over with Spanish chalk or whiting, after which the colours can be applied. Thirdly, when the painting is dry, heat should be applied, which would cause the wax to absorb the colours. The resulting paint surface would withstand the vagaries of the weather and, it was claimed, last longer than an oil. Although the colours do not have the rich gloss of an oil, the soft sheen-like finish may be viewed from any angle. The colours are quite secure and the account continues:

> and will bear washing; and have a property, which I look upon as the most important of any, which is, that they have smoaked this picture in places subject to foul vapours, and to smoke in chimnies; and then by being exposed to the dew, it became as clean as if it had been but just painted.

The claim above would seem to be ambitious, and not without risk. Unquestionably, if anyone had in their collection a wooden mummy painting from Fayum or another source, the use of water as a cleaning agent could very much put the picture in jeopardy in certain circumstances. The 18th-century publication goes on to describe the technique in detail and it is of interest to examine parts of it as an illustration of the intricacies of some of the painting methods of the past. Textiles as well as wood may be prepared for working on, and the instructions state that any sort of linen cloth may be used which should first be stretched upon a straining frame, similar to the stretcher used for oil painting canvas. Then the back of the canvas should be well rubbed with beeswax and care taken that a fair amount of the wax adheres to the cloth. For careful work it advises that the painting surface should be rubbed over with á piece of pumice stone which will remove knots and uneveness that could obstruct the free flow of the brush.

The writer also states that all colours used with oil painting may be used with this adventure into encaustic. He describes too how a form of wax crayon can be prepared with the colours, which for some artists may be a happier technique than the brush. His list of recommended pigments informs us about the complexities of the studio for some of the early painters. With the white, he talks about flake white, and white lead, or ceruse, making the remark that flake white alone is liable to raise little bubbles when used with water. He recommends the Venetian or Dalmatian white lead as by far the best for encaustic, followed by the German or Dutch, French or English ceruse. The yellows include: Naples, light ochre, brown ochre, yellow orpiment or King's yellow, and red orpiment. Naples yellow is suggested as the only colour for rendering the tenderer flesh tints of women. It continues with the statement that it can be very tender, bright and a beautiful-lasting colour for all manner of painting if properly prepared and managed; if not, it is a dirty, weak and treacherous one, particularly with oil. Naples yellow is a mineral compound of lead, antimony, sulphur, and some arsenic, which latter is the cause of its changing, and hurting other colours (possibly the artist as well), and particularly the white, so much complained of by the painters. The account then goes on with advice on how to clean a dirty and treacherous Naples yellow – as if the hard-worked assistant had not enough to do. Take crude Naples yellow and break it into small pieces with a mallet upon the grinding stone, put it in a clean earthen vessel, and pour over it a quantity of new milk, sufficient to cover it three or four inches over, stirring it well with a wooden spatula or stick. Then it should be allowed to stand and settle for five or six days. The milk will by that time become thick and sour, and by its acidity will absorb and cleanse the 'noxious saline principles of the colour'. After this the creamy top of the milk should be skimmed off and warm water should be poured into the vessel until it overflows and this should be continued until the water becomes quite clear.

The next colours mentioned are light pink and brown pink – which are made from a concoction of French berries and acid salts which, to be rendered usable with encaustic, should be mixed with a little light ochre. The reds include: lake, vermilion or cinnabar, minium or red-lead, light red or light ochre calcined, brown red or brown ochre calcined and Indian red. A warning with regard to the lake is given; this infers that the Florence lake, which is recommended as the best, is in general the worst, and is usually in small hard grains. This may be caused by the addition of gum arabic, or worse, the glutinous substance that oozes from the cherry tree, the substance being put in by the maker of the lake to give it the appearance of being better. Such lake will scale off canvas. Minium is strongly recommended as being the best red – rather overlooking the danger for the artist using it. Two earth colours are mentioned, *terra di Siena* and *terra verde*. The Siena is not advised for use with encaustic because the nature of its granulation does not allow the wax to penetrate properly. The *terra verde* is given a scathing report; it comes from Italy and Germany and should be banished from the palette because it grows dirty and black, particularly with oil, and is one of the causes of the flesh tints in early Italian paintings going black. Blues include ultramarine, Prussian and smalt; the Prussian being recommended for encaustic, as it is unlikely to darken. Blacks are ivory, bone and blue black; the last being praised for its texture, the pigment is made by calcining apricot, peach and plum-stones. It is suggested that the best bone black is made from calcined mutton trotters. Amongst the browns is Collen's earth, a name unknown today and one which should arouse suspicions as it is made from a bituminous earth and would be likely to give rise to many troubles after it was applied.

The crayon method for encaustic may be carried out on canvas, wooden panel or a plastered wall; the crayons being either in the form of a type of pastel in which the pigment is mixed with a small amount of pipe clay and bound with a few drops of weak casein or size, or crayons bound with a little bees-wax. Whichever support is used it will need to be waxed, the canvas from the back and the wooden panel or plaster from the front, heat is then applied to cause the materials to become impregnated with the wax. For anyone wishing to try crayon encaustic today, the heat may be applied by holding towards a fire or, better still, one of those hot-air electric paint strippers, if controlled carefully, will do the job very well. The technical term for this application of heat to the encaustic panel is to inust, using an inusting tool. Canvas supports may also be primed with a mixture of fine wheat flour or starch and water boiled up together with the addition, when it thickens, of a strange sub-stance called horse-turpentine. This is the kind of ingredient which appears in ancient recipes and can bring the whole attempt to a direct halt. In practice, whether working on canvas, wooden panel or plastered wall, it will be found helpful for the execution of the work if a thin coat of slightly gritty plaster is laid over the whole surface, if desired this can be tinted; the effect of this is to catch and drag away more colour from the crayon than a smoother priming. The fixing of the crayon encaustic is similar to the painted method, a thorough going over the surface of the picture with the inusting tool. After the whole has cooled down, the surface can be polished to a desired sheen with soft cloths. If a slightly higher gloss is preferred, or it is thought desirable to lay a toned glazed effect, this may be done with egg white which should be well worked into the paint surface. When dry, a thin picture varnish, either clear or with the chosen colour, should be brushed sparsely over the picture. As the varnish is laid over dried egg white, it should be simple to remove if a change is thought necessary at a later date.

Also in the 18th century a gentleman by the name of Werner of Neustadt tried to penetrate the secrets of encaustic. He pro-duced a wax emulsion that was water soluble by heating together white wax (presumably a highly purified beeswax) with potash at a ratio of one pound wax to one and a half pounds potash, the potash first being dissolved in water. As it cooled, the waxy emulsion floated to the surface in the form of a white saponaceous substance; when this was triturated with water an emulsion was produced which Werner called wax milk. This milk could be mixed with the whole range of colours suitable for encaustic and in every way worked very well. Towards the end of the century, a Mrs Hooker of Rottingdean made a number of experiments with methods of painting in and with wax and for these she received a gold palette from the Society of Arts. Her account of the techniques she worked on was printed in the 10th volume of the Society's Transactions 1792 under the name of Miss Emma Jane Greenland.

In Germany in the 19th century further experiments were carried out into encaustic and a considerable revival of interest by artists resulted. A natural resin such as damar was mixed with the beeswax, and this gave a harder finish and a more stable working quality – supports were limited to wooden panels or plastered walls because the movement of a textile would cause cracking. A method of mixing the wax with an oil gave a medium that could be painted on to canvas in the same way as a normal paint. The colours were mixed with the resin or oil and kept on a heated palette whilst the artist was working. After the painting was finished it was inusted in the usual way. Sometimes paraffin wax was used, but although it was judged quite stable it gave a difficult working quality to the paints. One slight snag from the painter's point of view is that with the oil medium, as the colours dry they tend to become lighter in tone, and it is very difficult to judge the final appearance. The use of wax intermixed with oils and varnishes for the oil technique can be fraught. It is possible that the poor state of some of Sir Joshua Reynolds' paintings may be because he injudiciously mixed wax with other ingredients whilst he was searching for his 'perfect' medium.

The range of pigments available for the painter was continually growing and often it is to that untiring recorder Pliny, who apparently even continued writing whilst being carried in a litter by his slaves, that one turns for information. Dragon's blood is a warm darkish resin that can be tapped from a number of trees, in particular the dragon tree; barely strong enough in tinting power to be a useful pigment it has done service with the preparation of varnishes and glazes. Pliny comes up with a marvellous description of its origin. He tells us that in India the dragon and the elephant are perpetually at war, in which each individual combat ends in a titanic tragedy; the elephant is strangled and crushed by the coils of the dragon and falls dead across the dragon who is annihilated by the huge weight of his foe; their mingled blood producing for us 'dragon's blood'. Pliny also comes up with a romantic fiction for 'cinnabar' which he tells is the proper name for the thick matter which issues from the body of the dragon and mixes with the blood of the elephant. As an art critic Pliny could at times get carried away with his own fantasies. One note records his reaction when comparing the simple palette used by the Greeks with the desire for brilliant colours by the Romans, which, whilst giving no pictures of high quality, results in 'India sending to Rome the slime of her rivers, and the corrupt blood of her dragons and elephants'. But in general descriptions of techniques, pigments and their sources are really very correct. His life must have been exciting: he was the Collector of the Imperial revenues in Spain, a close friend of Vespasian, and in the end he was in command of the fleet of Messina when Vesuvius erupted and buried Pompeii and Herculaneum. Pliny, despite his seventy-nine years, rushed to the scene of the disaster and succumbed in the suffocating and toxic fumes from the volcano.

Other colours that are described by Pliny include white lead and verdigris, and he would have known of massicot for instance. Massicot was prepared by melting lead, then either collecting the scum that forms on the surface of the molten metal or waiting until the whole molten mass is oxidised, when a pleasant yellow pigment is secured. This lasted as a favourite with painters at least until the 17th-century Dutch School. The Romans were great ones for using lead, most of their plumbing was carried out in this unpleasant metal. As well as massicot, a fine orange could be produced by roasting white lead. White lead itself was prepared from lead grids and vinegar – a nasty process for the operative. The stack of lead sheets and the vinegar were placed under a tan from a tannery, the acid vapour attacking the lead, and carbonic acid gas being given off by the fermentation, until finally the lead was converted into lead carbonate. The whole process took several weeks. Verdigris was produced in a slightly similar manner from copper sheets which were buried in grape skins from the wine vats until the metal was turned into acetate of copper.

Indigo was known, both the variety from India and the substance obtained from the dyers' vats in which woad had been prepared. Other dyes included weld, Persian berries, kermes, madder and possibly Indian lac. And there was of course the Imperial or Tyrian purple, an essential colour for the proud conquering hero from Rome; both Pliny and Vitruvius described this rather splendid colour. The pigment is produced by a number of shellfish round the shores of the Mediterranean. The most sought after were *Murex brandaris* and *Murex trunculus*. These hapless creatures must have been dredged up in huge numbers; large piles of broken shells have been discovered close to the ancient ports of Tyre and Sidon. The shells were broken open and a small sac cut out; this is colourless initially but when it is exposed to the sun it turns first yellow, then green, followed by a slightly bluish tint and finally a strong, deep purple. Apart from robing the Romans, Tyrian purple remained a standby for illuminated manuscripts until the 17th century. The pigment as a dye was remarkably resistant to fading and was insoluble in acetic acid. Even under modern testing it remains insoluble in alcohol and ether and only gives way a little with boiling benzene.

Just as the exact process of encaustic has caused much argument, so has the technique used by the painters at Pompeii and Herculaneum. The work was carried out over a period of about three hundred years, although basically it would appear to be the same approach throughout. The most noticeable feature with these remarkable murals is the subtle reflecting sheen which they possess even today. The accomplishment of these early artists, not only technically but also aesthetically, is impressive even when measured against any period of art that was to follow. Various experts have suggested that the paintings are basically *fresco* or *secco* or a form of encaustic – but none of these really fits with their unique appearance.

Ernst Berger was the first (in 1904) to pronounce that the murals were worked in what is termed '*stucco lustro*'. The complete technique cannot even now be accurately described but the following is probably approximately correct. The grounding must have been all important, this could have been layered with a first application of coarse river sand with rich lime, then a second coat of sand and lime, but with sand of a much finer grain. Then came three layers of stucco composed of marble dust and lime which had been well sieved, the last two layers being smoothed down with a wooden float. Finally the colours would be applied, mixed with a pure soap and potash, thus being easy and fluid to use. When dry, the surface would have been ironed with low heat, that which is just bearable to the hand, and within a few hours the ironing would have been repeated to force the colours into the top layer of the stucco. Then after a period of several weeks the surface would be given a light coating of warm turpentine and beeswax, the excess being mopped off. Last would be a thorough polishing with soft cloths.

The command that these painters had not only over their technique but also over the indicating of light and shade, and the feeling towards a form of perspective which gave their works a remarkable sensation of the third dimension, is almost startling.

Figurative realism as seen in the panel in the House of the Vettii, Pompeii, which shows the infant Hercules strangling serpents, has a verve and vitality which was not matched for hundreds of years. As well as the panels of mural painting there was much decorative architectural detail suggested with consummate skill. The stifling volcanic dust which turned to mud over the two doomed cities did bring a latent blessing. Much detail and many everyday objects were kept intact until the archeologist's spade could reach them. A paint shop in Pompeii was found with samples of the pigments which the painters would have used; they had been carefully ground up and stored in small jars.

It is unlikely that collectors will possess, in the same way as museums, examples of the foregoing, with the possible exception of the mummy paintings; but it can increase the appreciation of such works to know something of the pains the artists and craftsmen took. Man had by now rejected ideas of totally blank walls around him, and the cartographic recording of the Egyptians was replaced by the advance of an aesthetic conception to enrich life. Some Roman examples are almost *trompe l'oeil* in the way perspective is handled to give an idea of greater space to a room, also in the lifelike representation of decorative details. Surveying the vault of the Tomb of Pancratii in Rome, which was carried out in a form of fresco and stucco, it is hard to believe that the date of execution was AD 150; or that the glowing warmth and intricate detail of the *cubiculum* of the Villa of P. Fannius Sinistor, Boscoreale (removed to the Metropolitan Museum, New York) was worked in the 1st century BC.

Principally about Tempera and Illumination

One of the most confusing terms in painting can be tempera, many collectors are unsure as to its exact meaning. As a collective term it implies a method of painting in which the pigments are mixed with a water medium, an emulsion or water-soluble glue. Variations of the medium were certainly used by the Greeks and some of the paintings on textiles of the early Egyptians can be classed as a form of tempera. Pictures painted in this way may occur on textiles of varying types, wooden panels, cards, papers and ceramic plaques. Attempts may well have been made on metal sheets, although the character of the tempera paint film with whatever binding medium would be unsympathetic to adhering to the metal. The natural appearance of the dried paint surface is a mat sheen, but over the years the paintings may have been varnished. In this case they will have the look of a smoothly painted oil; varnishing also tends to darken certain pigments, notably the blues, greens and browns.

The binding substances that have been mixed with the dry pigments over the past two thousand years can include any one and sometimes two or more of the following: size prepared by boiling down cuttings of parchment, whole eggs, egg whites, egg yolks, fig milk, cherry tree gum, certain waxes, fish-glue, gum tragacanth, gum arabic, glycerine, honey, milk and sundry other substances which may have taken the whim of the experimenting artist and probably brought an early demise for his paintings.

For the purist tempera would have been and still is egg yolk only, perhaps with a very small amount of preservative, a few drops of acetic acid is effective. Certainly the pigments when mixed with just the yolk dry out with that almost indefinable subtle silk-like sheen that is the great attraction of the medium. The eggs need to be as fresh as possible and care is needed with the separation of the yolks. Step one is to crack the egg and allow the white to pour off, then roll the yolk in its sac around in the palms of the hands to remove traces of the white. Now with great gentleness pick up the sac between thumb and forefinger, hold it over a suitable container and stab the underside with a clean sharp blade to allow the pure yolk to pour out, then discard the sac. The pigments can then be ground into or mixed with the yolk; small quantities of pure water can be mixed in if it is desired to thin down the paint. Medieval painters generally appear to have painted with their tempera quite freely diluted. Cennino Cennini, who wrote in *Il Libro dell'Arte* (c. 1400), the most important treatise in the history of painting, mentions seven, eight or ten coats being applied to achieve the desired depths or nuances of tone and tint. The egg tempera film is extraordinarily permanent, being unlikely to crack, flake or blister even under conditions which would upset an oil painting; additionally it should pose few problems for the professional picture restorer when a cleaning is called for. The principal safety feature is to ensure that such a painting does not hang in a damp, stagnant atmosphere, and to inspect for mould growths. Care should be taken that it is protected where possible from abrasion, this can be done by glazing or having a fairly deep-set frame.

Apart from panel pictures, egg tempera features with *fresco secco* which is dealt with in the following chapter. The preparation of the panel in past centuries called for much patience and dedicated work in the studio. The basic grounding on the wood, which would have to be properly seasoned, was *gesso*; this substance is broadly a mixture of a plaster and a glue, and it features not only in painting but also with a number of the craftsman's skills, gilded furniture, gilded mirrors, lacquered surfaces, and situations where it is necessary to provide a stable base for a highly finished applied surface. The recipes for the making of *gesso* are various and many artists have their own pet ingredients. The ideal finished surface of the panel should have the smoothness of polished marble and a hardness that would resist the scratching of a finger nail. Cennini makes much reference to the preparation and grounding of panels, underlining the need for care and explaining how, if modelling for raised details is needed, tow may be mixed in with the *gesso*.

One ancient recipe for the making of *gesso* which really works extremely well if plenty of time is available is this: overslake plaster of Paris for three weeks and leave a quantity of milk to sour for the same time. Pour off the surplus water from the plaster of Paris and strain out the junket-like curd from the soured milk. Take three parts of the plaster and one part of sour curd, mix together and gently warm in a double container, raise the temperature to about as hot as can be borne by the hand and the *gesso* will be ready to use.

A simple and thoroughly effective recipe can be to prepare a size from rabbit-skin glue – two ounces of the glue dissolved in half a pint of water – heat in a double container and then stir in enough whiting to give the consistency desired.

The preparation of a *gesso* panel is carried out in this way. The wooden panel may be of a number of woods, beech, ash, oak, poplar have been used, as have some of the pines. The main points are that the timber should be thoroughly seasoned, not too absorbent and fairly hard. The first step is to attach a piece of scrim, muslin or thinly-woven linen cloth with a strong size. Then a stiffish *gesso* should be prepared, this is known as *grosso*; apply to the panel to a depth of about 3–6 mm (⅛–¼ of an inch), level this off as well as possible with a broad bristle brush. Leave to set for forty-eight hours. Now prepare a thinner mixture, *gesso sottile*, and before applying to the panel, strain through some fine mesh to be sure that no lumps are left. Again apply with a brush of softish hair; the consistency of the warm *gesso sottile* should be something like double cream. Two or more coats can be applied, allowing twenty-four hours at least between each. To get the *gesso sottile* to really level out it can sometimes help to gently tap the panel underneath and around the edges. Again leave for a period to harden out and then rub the surface with varied grades of pumice block to achieve that feel of smooth ivory.

The applying of egg tempera has certain vagaries which have discouraged some painters. It can be difficult to judge the final dried-out tint of some pigments when mixed with the egg and also a number of pigments, particularly the earths, need care with mixing, different amounts of egg yolk being called for to achieve the right consistency. The mixture needs to have just enough fluidity for easy flow from the brush, if it is too thick the pigment can pile up an unsightly impasto which has no part with the egg tempera technique.

After the *gesso* panel has been satisfactorily smoothed down, some painters might prefer to lay a thin veiling or imprimatura of a tint such as burnt umber, burnt sienna or *terre verte*; this would be done with the colour tempered with the egg yolk and a fairly liberal amount of water. Tempera pictures exist which have the luminous and transparent appearance of water colour, these will have been painted with a considerable dilution of water to the mixture; some will be found with the look of gouache, and this would indicate amounts of white being added to the colours during the mixing. There are also numerous examples from the Byzantine period where the paint film may well resemble a flat oil; the artists had added different oils and, in a number of cases, this has caused the pictures to yellow and darken. Certainly, egg tempera at its finest should not be adulterated with oils, waxes or varnishes, for only in this way can that peerless purity of the pure yolk-bound film be safeguarded.

The initial drawing-in can be by weak-toned brush strokes of a neutral colour, or pencil or, if the composition is large and complicated, the roulette and pounce method may be employed. With this last a cartoon or outline is prepared on a thin tough paper similar to tracing paper. Then the paper is laid on a soft support and the roulette is run over the lines; the wheel will leave behind a succession of tiny holes. Next the cartoon is laid on top of the wooden gesso-covered panel and some powdered graphite or charcoal is put into two or three thicknesses of muslin, folded over to form a round ball, and this is pounced or dapped along the lines. Little dots of graphite will be deposited on the gesso as guides for the painter. The same transference method is used by the mural painter.

One feature of tempera painting that has to be mastered is the speed with which the colours dry out once they are applied to the panel; to a lesser degree this will also happen with the colours on the palette, thus only small amounts should be mixed up as the work progresses. The brushwork should have a precision and the painter should realise that an even film should be aimed for – thick enough to achieve opaque effects when needed – but not too thick or the colours will tend to flake. If some of the Old Masters' work is studied, it will be seen that they used a hatching technique for rendering depth and volume. Other artists might first build up a modelled monochrome over the initial drawing, then aim to work up the picture by laying one coat of the colour over another rather in the manner of transparent water colour. This method can be effective and will certainly appear freer, but it will have to be done rapidly owing to the speed of drying of the tempera films – no attempt should be made to scumble and push the colours around with a finger tip as the painter in oils might do – it will only end in disaster with an unpleasant and fractured paint film. The painter must also remember the whole time he is working that colours can change quite considerably as they dry out. This unfortunately is not consistent right across the palette. Yellows and reds will tend to lighten only a little, earth browns a great deal, dark blues like Prussian very little, paler blues a good deal, as will most greens. To try and control this feature and also the speed of drying, some painters have been tempted to add substances akin to honey or plant juices – this may work, but the finished painting will not have that elusive beauty of the true egg tempera, combining an almost ethereal feeling with near transparency and the unique delicate strength of the colours. Sandro Botticelli shows he is a master of this medium with his group of the 'Three Graces' in his large panel 'Allegory of Spring' in the Uffizi in Florence. Worked in this manner, egg tempera can give a method of expression for the painter that is not otherwise possible.

In the 15th century particularly, painters working under Guild rulings and with time provided by their patrons could spend long periods on extra enrichment of their work. One example of this is by the use of gold leaf as part of the background or as a complete grounding almost in the way of an imprimatura. At times a rather dull and strange looking 'gold' has been used, this is likely to be tin leaf which would have been covered with a coat of yellow varnish as a cheap substitute for the gold. Silver leaf was also used in the same way, but both will give trouble, the silver can blacken with tarnish and the tin is liable to disintegrate. Pure gold leaf is a delightful experience to work over; the richness of the 'king of metals' can do wonderful things with the colours, notably alizarin crimson, cobalt blue, viridian and others that are highly transparent. The preparation of the leaves is a considerable craft on its own. Roll out the metal or beat it flat but still keep it fairly thick and it is called sheet metal. Reduce it to the thickness of newsprint and it is termed foil. Now continue the thinning process until the gold has about as much substance as a spider's web, with pratically no weight and almost the beginnings of transparency and it is then leaf. Few metals have the malleable quality that will allow them to be beaten thinner than foil, but with gold the beater can go on and on. The extremely thin leaves are of little use for the arts because they are to all intents and purposes transparent, and so frail as to be well-nigh impossible to handle. Cennini has much to say on the subject and gives some idea of the area a quite small amount of gold could be made to cover. The goldbeater of his day could beat 145 leaves out of a ducat (the Venetian gold ducat weighed 54 Troy grains); which makes a single leaf weigh around 0.37, although the scribe feels that this is too thin for the painter and that not more than a hundred leaves should come from a ducat. It is likely that the leaf size then was about eight and a half centimetres square; so one ducat of gold could cover an area of about 50 odd square feet.

The laying of the leaf itself was a skilled matter. The *gesso* would first be given an underlyng ground of a red earth, a bole, often the one termed Armenian; this would be mixed to a workable consistency, probably with a little egg white, and when it was dried the adhesive for the leaf would be brushed thinly over the surface. There were a number of recipes for this but one standby seems to have been glair, which was egg white well beaten up with a little water. Then the gold leaf would be picked up on a broad soft-hair brush known as a 'tip' and laid in position; each sheet was normally given a lap of about a quarter of an inch. Decorative work with patterned punches could be applied before the glair or other adhesive had completely hardened. After several days the gold would be stable, and if desired areas could be given a particular enrichment and sparkle with the careful use of an agate burnisher. Some of the artists would even go so far as to create a form of arched window effect; when this was done the *gesso* would generally be reinforced with animal hair or tow.

Another method for applying gold was to reduce it to a powder, mix it with the egg yolk or other vehicle and use it as a paint. The trouble with grinding gold is that it has such an extreme quality of malleability that, even when cut up into small pieces for grinding, it will tend to self-weld. The medieval craftsman is reported as getting round this difficulty by grinding the gold with honey which would keep the particles separate. Then, when the needed fineness of powder was reached the honey could be washed away quite easily with warm water. In medieval records there is mention of another way for using gold. This is ingenious – the painter would cover the area with a substance like powdered glass or some fine hard grit mixed with a fixing medium. When this had hardened it had a surface like fine sandpaper; into this could then be rubbed a lump of gold which would be abraded and leave quite considerable traces behind. Both this method and the powdered gold paint could be worked on with burnishers.

A further thought on the use of gold leaf and die stamping with paintings is that often the same type of pattern or dies can be recognised in different paintings. If these are highly individual, it can help with authentication because it could indicate that the pictures are likely to have come from the same workshop.

With early religious painting there was often a certain amount of symbolism attached to or associated with the principal figures; very often gold leaf was used to underline such features, and was laid for haloes or crowns and similar accents. From the 15th century onwards there was a whole language of symbolism in paintings which can be fascinating to trace; nearly always confined to religious subjects, it was possibly ordered by ecclesiastical patrons to strengthen the intended message. Animals, birds and insects featured: a butterfly was the symbol of the Resurrection, a camel signified temperance, a crane meant vigilance and loyalty, a partridge stood for the Church and truth. Plants included the almond for divine approval, the cherry for sweet character, the dandelion implied the Passion, the lemon stood for fidelity and the willow for the gospel of Christ. The symbolism included other subjects for earth and sky, the Virgin Mary, Jesus Christ, the Trinity, the Saints and religious objects.

Picture making is an exciting subject to study as it unfolds: there were practical difficulties of materials and techniques to be overcome. During the 15th century and the following years, many of the peaks of accomplishment were being assailed. Constant efforts were being made to discover the true secret of showing the third dimension on a two-dimensional working area; for although the early Roman painters had gone a long way towards this, their skills, like many others, were lost sight of in the so-called Dark Ages. Witness the efforts of Giotto working away at the problem of perspective with his 'Pentecost' (now in the National Gallery, London) and Uccello with his 'Rout of San Romano' (in the same gallery), here he hopefully drapes corpses and weapons at angles that indicate some imagined vanishing point. Those twin miracles of light and shade were gradually being understood by artists, examine works by Rembrandt, Wright of Derby, Georges de La Tour and Caravaggio to glimpse how much the trained and seeking eye of the painter can lead the viewer into seeing things never noticed before. Colours available for the artist were increasing, and those vital tools the brushes were improving in quality.

The sometimes strange materials that have been tried for brush-making almost rival those called in by the colourman. Hairs and bristles from animal sources include badger, fitch, civet, ermine, goat, ox-ear, ringcat, pony, horse, racoon, bear, squirrel and kolinsky sable. The last is the chosen one for the finest of all brushes. The guard hairs from the tail of this small weasel-like animal are most suitable, being strong and resilient, also the shape, with a slight bellying in the centre of the hairs, greatly assists in giving a highly workable brush head which holds the colour well and is accurate with the strokes. Sable

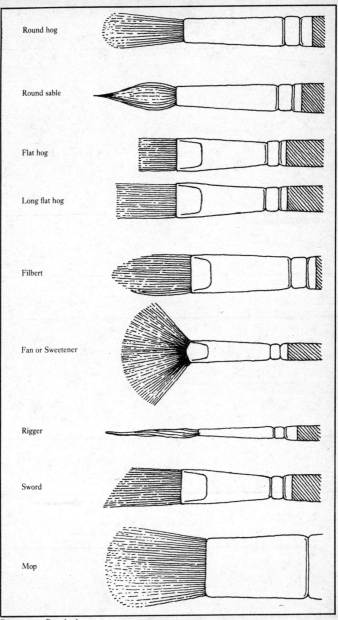

Round hog

Round sable

Flat hog

Long flat hog

Filbert

Fan or Sweetener

Rigger

Sword

Mop

Diagram 1 Brush shapes

brushes are used principally with water colour and tempera. Some attempts have been made to use human hair, but they have not been successful. Reasonably good brushes have been made from baleen. Bristles for oil painting brushes come from the pig, hog or boar, those from the back and shoulders being the most suitable. Apparently the best animals are those that are somewhere between the wild boar and the domestic pig. Seventeenth-century Russia was a plentiful supplier, and there are records stating that in 1640 a ½d duty should be paid for each 12lbs of Russian bristle entering London docks. China was one of the great producers of bristle, although mostly black and not the preferred white; early in the 20th century the Chinese pig population was put at over 55,000,000 from which the farmers could hope to harvest about 10,000,000lbs of bristle.

Vegetable fibres have also been used, harking back to the early Egyptians with their date palm fibre. Examples include agave, yucca, tampico fibre from Mexico, sisal, bass, coco fibre, certain grasses and twigs of heather, tamarisk and Spanish broom. Today gradual progress is being made with synthetic fibres but there is a long way to go before they can equal the working qualities of sable and fine bristle. To the artist his brush is a most sensitive tool: it must combine strength with subtlety and help to pass on his inspiration with as little trouble as possible.

Over the years a number of different brush shapes have been evolved, each of which can give the painter particular characteristics of stroke produced by their shapes. Almost certainly the round brush was the first, and this has been followed by short and long flat shapes; the filbert, which is a marriage of the round and flat; the rigger with its long fine sable hairs; the fan or sweetener for blending; the sword, useful for long curving lines; and large round and flat bushy soft-hair wash-brushes. All the finest of these are made by hand by dedicated craftsmen. It needs years of experience to be able to pick up just the right amount of hair or bristle for a certain shape or size, and then to bind and set the brush heads in the metal ferrules on the handles. In earlier centuries soft-hair brushes were often set in quills which would serve as ferrules and sometimes as handles as well. Those from the water fowl were recommended, the large feathers from geese or swans being in demand. For fine work, a number of painters would choose the tiny pointed flight feathers from teal, widgeon or woodcock, and these stuck into an old brush handle still serve well today.

The story of picture-making does not proceed in an orderly

manner with clearly divided areas of progress because the principal methods employed all tend to overlap one another – not only historically but often, to an extent, with the techniques. Nor is it possible to give an exact date when a particular method started or which painter was first to use that method. Tempera in one or other of its forms was evolved during the Dynasties of the Pharaohs and is still being used today. Sometimes there are patches of time when a technique will seem to have been obliterated, then it returns. Artists and craftsmen have an urge to express; the flame of that expression carries through against oppression and discouragement. When the break-up of the Western Roman Empire came, it was a wrenching, cruel time. The imposed culture of the Romans cracked and broke under the tumultuous surge of the Barbarians that poured from the vast unknown of the East. Somehow the tenuous thread of civilisation was kept alive by the monasteries, which became not only the centres for the promulgation of the Christian faith but also places where the traditions of the artistic crafts could be practised. Many artists' hands were needed to decorate the churches as paeans of praise to God, many more were required to bring into being the glories of the illuminated manuscript. To gaze at some of the manuscripts is to wonder at the technique, the genius that, coupled with a timeless patience, let these lonely men produce what in many cases are miracles of invention, decoration and supreme examples of the handling of materials.

Illumination in art is a term that implies the embellishment of a written or printed text; the old form of the verb 'to illuminate' was 'to enlumine' which comes from the Old French *enluminer* literally implying to throw light on. The practice of decorating texts with pictorial representations goes back unquestionably as far as fifteen centuries BC when the Egyptians produced 'The Book of the Dead' which contains numerous scenes painted in bright and clean colours. Accounts by early Latin writers show that illustrated books were not uncommon in Rome, certainly in the first part of the empire. Among the threads that bridge the fall of the Roman Empire to the Middle Ages are a few surviving manuscripts, probably the oldest of which is a fragmentary copy of the *Iliad* which is in the Ambrosian Library at Milan. It is likely that it was worked in Italy during the 3rd century – there appears to be some influence from the talented wall paintings at Pompeii, and also from those in the catacombs. There is also the Vatican Virgil, the *Schedae Vaticanae*, dating from the 4th century. These are the roots from which grew the golden age of the illuminator which culminated in such sublime masterpieces as the Lindisfarne Gospels, c.700, The Book of Kells, 8th century, which today rests as the glory of Trinity College Library, Dublin, and the magnificent Book of Hours of the Duc de Berry which was produced by the Limbourg brothers in the early years of the 15th century. For an example of graphic reporting by a painterly scribe, the *Valerius Maximus* worked about 1475 by Philippe de Comines would be difficult to better; a whole grisly story from some happening in medieval times etches itself into the memory by the sheer skill and story-telling power of its executor.

How did they make these manuscripts which sometimes had a surpassing loveliness and at others a cold cruelty, but always the technique of masters? The recognised material or support on which to work was either parchment or vellum. These terms can be confusing; broadly, parchment is prepared from the skin of a goat or sheep and vellum from the skin of a calf – although parchment does in many senses include vellum. The preparation of parchment in the Middle Ages was carried out by specialists who probably had private recipes which would not be imparted to the scribes. But an outline treatment would have consisted first of soaking the skins in water to clean them and then transferring them to a bath of lime and water to loosen the hair; this process could take several days. After this the wool and hair could be easily rubbed and pulled off, the lime would also remove much of the fat and oil. Subsequently the skins would be stretched on frames to dry. Some of the finest parchment was produced in Bologna in the 13th century, where the practice was to give a second lime bath followed by two days in ample supplies of fresh clean water. Parchment skins are liable to shrink considerably when drying, so the business of stretching has to be done with care. During the initial stages of the stretching whilst the skins were good and wet they had to be scraped with a moon-shaped knife which was called a *lunellarium*. If a skin was particularly fat and oily, alkalis, ashes and lime would be applied to draw out this mess. The hardness of some of the 15th-century parchments is probably because they were given a dressing of alum. If a parchment exhibits a spotty or blotchy appearance it is likely that it was not fresh at the time it was treated. Lesser qualities of the precious material were probably made from the skins of animals such as deer, and that for the pages of the smaller books may well have been prepared from the skins of rabbits or squirrels.

With a well-treated parchment, it would have been possible to work on it as soon as it was dry, but it is more likely that the surface could still have retained some grease, and it would need to have a careful rubbing down with pumice powder or pumice blocks, chalk or colophony – a dark resin made from the residue of distilled turpentine usually termed 'rosin'. English workers of the period saved themselves the cost of importing the pumice by making up a rather strange type of bread; this consisted of a fearsome dough made from brewers' yeast, flour and water plus a fair amount of powdered glass. This mass was allowed to rise and then baked in the oven. Just another of the occupational hazards of being a medieval craftsman if this loaf got stored in the kitchen bin!

Some workers sought to assist the adherence of the colours by priming the areas to be decorated with a form of water-soluble glue; others would give several coats of dilute white lead oil paint.

With illuminating work, the most important vehicle for binding the pigments was glair (see page 29). Once again there is evidence of the almost endless pains the medieval craftsman would take. The preparing of glair is discussed in an 11th-century manuscript 'De clarea' which is in Berne. The information includes the fact that there are two kinds of glair, one of which is made by beating and the other, weaker and more brittle, by pressing; the latter can also be contaminated, having been repeatedly squeezed through cloth or wool, and therefore having picked up dirt from the hand of the person carrying out the operation. The writer goes on to say that for that reason glair should always be very cleanly handled.

Undoubtedly, the preparation of glair does take a long time; it is vital also that the bowl and beating implements are scrupulously clean – any contamination will bring down the colours and might even encourage mould growths and staining later. The finished glair should be smooth and snowy white, and quite even in texture. Insufficient beating of the glair can prove a pitfall to many; if it is whipped too little it will almost resemble a glue and when mixed with the colour will make it stringy.

Once the glair was thoroughly beaten up to the light snowy froth it would be left to stand and liquefy. The second problem facing the painter was that the egg white and water mixture would go bad fairly soon. To prevent this a small amount of realgar – red sulphide of arsenic – or a few drops of vinegar were added. It was essential, also, to keep air away from the glair, for if it was left even a short time, it would very quickly dry out.

Some workers liked to use a mixture of gum arabic and glair and this could be beneficial because the gum arabic would serve to make a more resistant film or paint. One of the most interesting materials used by medieval painters and possibly by Arab counterparts was garlic juice. This has been tested, and it certainly is a highly suitable binder for pigments. It can also be used as an adhesive with gold leaf and other materials employed by the illuminator. The process of collecting it is somewhat arduous. The cloves of garlic need to be skinned and then put through a press; next the juice will have to be sieved to remove any stringy matter or lumps. Kept in an airtight bottle, garlic juice has a long life without any additive to preserve it. It is a fine clear liquid to work with and brushes out with ease; also it has another advantage when gilding, that is, if it has dried recently it will become sticky again when gently breathed on.

Today much gilding is done using gold size; there are a number of different versions concocted by proprietary makers. The paste for the raising of gold and other ornaments can be made using any of the mordants above; the powder may be fine marble dust, whiting or similar substances. The raising mixture should be of a consistency that can be readily used with a brush. Some users liked to have it quite liquid when they first traced out the designs, then a thicker consistency which would just drop off the brush and could be controlled would be used for subsequent layers. Raising pastes should have the characteristic mentioned above of becoming sticky when breathed upon if they have once dried out, so that they will receive the gold or other leaf.

The process for laying the leaf was close to the following. The raising paste is laid and then left for about ten minutes or until it reaches the right condition. Next, a piece of gold leaf slightly larger than the object is cut and, breathing upon it gently, is laid in place with the 'tip' or, if very small, with a narrow blade or small brush; if breathed on again it should at once adhere to the raising paste. Now it should be left for about an hour, by which time it will have properly hardened and any loose pieces can be removed with a soft brush. If the leaf has not adhered satisfactorily and there are areas missing, it is possible to have a second attempt; brush over with a liquid raising mixture, pause, and then lay another piece of gold leaf.

The full list of colours used by these perfectionists could fill a volume but it is fascinating to look at a selection.

One of the most notable was a black ink which was used not only by the monks for their manuscripts but also by painters working on gesso panels. For these the ink was diluted to give a light- toned liquid for drawing in subjects prior to painting. The blacks available during the medieval times included carbon black, which would have been similar to that used by the early Egyptians, and there was also an organic salt of iron which was pale at first, but blackened after use. A powerful rich black could also be obtained from the gallnuts on oak trees; these gallnuts contain tannic acid which can be recovered from them by soaking and then, if an iron salt is added, the black is produced. The scribes also used a range of black and dark greys made by grinding up various charcoals; willow and vine were popular making what was considered by some as the best, the *nigrum optimum*. The making of charcoal was a serious business, for if the twigs and wood fragments were not correctly treated and the process incomplete, the resulting pigment could have a brown cast. Thus accounts mention the vine twigs being placed in sealed casserole pots and being heated under careful supervision.

Other substances that could produce satisfactory blacks were almond shells and peach stones which would be charred rather as wood is for producing charcoal – peach black may still be found on some colourmen's lists today. The illuminators however, never seemed to have made use of ivory and bone blacks which were known to the ancients – a strange omission.

Another point of interest is that there is little mention or sign of use of the natural earth colours such as the umbers and the darker ochres. These pigments were used – perhaps almost by accident or availability – by the cavemen, but then seem to have dropped from view, possibly because the painters were seeking brightness and were not drawn to such colours, which have a rather low and dull tint value. But come the Renaissance, raw burnt umber, raw and burnt sienna, yellow ochre and the like became very much a part of the artist's palette, and have remained so ever since. Illuminators had no need to explore the subtleties of shadows, as did the painters who succeeded them.

The most important white was made from lead in the manner that is explained in the previous chapter; as this lead white reacted with some pigments such as verdigris, Cennini states: 'Take care never to get it near any white lead, for they are mortal enemies in every respect.' Thus efforts were made to find a white that would not attack such pigments and some better results came from the calcining of bones. Cennini explains:

You must know what bone is good. Take bone from the

> second joints and wings of fowls, or of a capon; and the older they are the better. Just as you find them under the dining-table, put them into the fire; when you see they have turned whiter than ashes, draw them out, and grind them well on the porphyry. . . .

Porphyry is an extremely hard rock that appears to have first been quarried in ancient Egypt and made excellent palettes or grinding slabs for the painter.

Under the heading of red came at times a fearsome selection. One of the favourites was, sadly for the longevity of the scribe, red lead or minium which has already been mentioned; it was that pigment which Pliny enthused over as 'flame colour' regardless of its lethal nature. An interesting point is that *miniare* implies working with minium, from this the craftsman so employed was known as a *miniator* and his products were *miniatura*. Other reds included cinnabar which is a naturally occurring mercury sulphide, deposits of which occur in Spain and also near Siena in Italy. Naturally occurring vermilion was produced from cinnabar; Cennini somewhat sinisterly remarking:

> This colour is made by alchemy, prepared in a retort. I am leaving out the system for this, because it would be too tedious to set forth in my discussions all the methods and receipts.

As beautiful a pigment as vermilion is it does have a snag, it can darken unpredictably when being used in certain ways and when up against other neighbouring pigments. Today it has been to a large extent replaced by cadmium red, although this modern, safe, manufactured pigment never quite matches the extremely subtle tone of vermilion which breathes out the slightest of pale blue nuances.

The monk illustrators had an imaginative supply of other reds from many sources. The lakes which could range in tint from warm orange to deep blue crimsons were from plant saps, berry juices and from some insects that would have been feeding on specific plants. A number of these delightful colours had a fair degree of permanence, others would fade. Ivy was renowned as a producer of a rich blood red; early scribes describe the method of obtaining the colour and this involved the stabbing of ivy stems in the springtime. The colour, however, is elusive because attempts have been made to extract it but without success – probably with time and much repeating the name of the plant may have become confused. After minium the most important red was grain, which is again a substance that causes confusion. It is an insect dye and is often mixed up with its near neighbours kermes and cochineal, both also from insects. Although in demand, these colours are still prone to fade. Another standby was, and still is, madder, a delicate warm crimson that could be extracted from the root of the plant; today it is made synthetically from alizarin, although some water colourists insist on obtaining natural madder because, strive as chemists do, they have not completely captured the delicate carnation which the genuine colour can impart. Dragon's blood also featured, as mentioned on page 20.

The most outstanding blue the monks possessed was ultramarine, produced from the semi-precious stone lapis lazuli; it remained on the shopping lists of painters through the Renaissance, gradually becoming more and more expensive. A substitute known as French ultramarine was produced in 1826, although as with the substitutes for madder and vermilion it does not quite reproduce the delicate casts of the true ultramarine, which the picture conservator soon realises when having to apply a retouch to a painting of the earlier periods. Cennini goes at length into the preparation of the pigment:

> Ultramarine blue is a colour illustrious, beautiful, and most perfect, beyond all other colours ... you want to recognise the good stone, choose that which you see is richest in blue colour.

This remark is because the rock bearing the ultramarine can have varying amounts of grey matter with it. He then goes on to state how it should be pounded in a mortar and worked up on the porphyry slab, sifted and pounded again, the more the better, to bring up the finest quality of colour. The powdered pigment should be mixed with pine resin, gum mastic and an unspecified wax, the doughy lump should be kneaded, then left for three days and worked again. Next in the lengthy prescription, the mass should be kneaded with rounded sticks in a bowl of warm lye – repeatedly straining off the lye which would be extracting the blue, allowing the pigment to settle and then pouring off the lye. Finally clean water is poured in to wash the colour, then drained off so that the powdered pigment can dry out. Other blues to help out included indigo, woad obtained from the *isatis tinctoria*, turnsole which, according to some medieval writings, was extracted from the seeds of the *crozophora*, the juice being recovered by pieces of cloth when pressure was applied. There were also a number of copper blues, including the strangely named blue bice. Purples included archil, which could have been obtained from various types of lichen, and the shell colours akin to Tyrian purple.

Malachite and verdigris featured as two of the more important greens and then there were several that came from plants. Under this heading are sap green from buckthorn berries, iris green from the juice of iris flowers – possibly a little alum was used to sterilise it. There were also greens made from the leaves of deadly nightshade and another from honeysuckle berries. Yellows included the paler and brighter versions of yellow ochre, orpiment already mentioned and realgar, also massicot, the manufacture of which is described on page 21. Under the heading of colours used in attempts to imitate gold come bile, which was probably first used by the Greeks, *aurum musicum*, a sulphide of tin, which is better known as mosaic gold, and the strong tinting dye saffron, which is extracted from the crocus. The 14th-century scribe from Northern France Master Peter of St Omer makes it clear how important it was to choose the right blooms.

> For there is a certain plant similar to the white one in its leaves and roots, the flowers of which we call crocus, but the laity call it saffron. When you observe that these flowers have certain brightness on one side at the top, you may know that it is not good. When you wet two fingers with saliva and rub the flower between them a little bit and you get your finger yellow from it immediately, you may know that it comes from Italy or Spain, and it is good.

Isidore of Seville apparently knew of another crocus, a better kind he thought, this was called Corycian, which probably was to be found in Cilicia.

Cennini speaks of the yellow as:

> A colour which is made from a herb called saffron . . .put it on a linen cloth, over a hot stone or brick. Then take half a goblet or glass full of good strong lye. Put the saffron in it; work it up on the slab . . . if you want to make the most perfect grass colour imaginable, take a little verdigris and some saffron. . .

Another delightful yellow was also obtained from a plant, this was from weld, a rather larger relative of the domestic garden mignonette; and rather late on the scene of illuminating came fustic, from the plant *chlorophora tinctoria*. Fustic arrived in Europe in the 16th century from the West Indies and Central America, but there is little evidence of its use, although it could have been incorporated with lacquer or resin to brush over silver and tin leaves to simulate gold.

Many of the illuminated capitals, notably with the Lindisfarne Gospels and The Book of Kells, are wonderful lessons in the art of space filling with design – they are worth studying if only to marvel at the invention of motifs by these early artists.

Illuminated works, whether in separate sheets – which in many cases are from dismembered volumes – or still in their original bindings, should be handled with great care – do not hurry the turning of pages – watch that they do not scuff one against the other. Some of the work from the east Mediterranean can be very fragile, the colours being all too slightly bound with a mordant and the gold leaf over-thin, or the adhesive used can have deteriorated. Works on parchment or vellum must at all costs be protected from damp, which will not only cause the sheets to distort but will also very quickly upset the adherence of colours and any metallic leaves used. If the bindings include leather on wood boards, inspect for woodworm and also, if kept in a dry air-conditioned atmosphere, watch out for the firebrat, a tiny insect that has a good appetite for glues and other related substances. If trouble is noticed, send as soon as possible for a specialist conservator.

The Painters of Walls
and Ceilings

The history of mural painting, the ability to compose on the often huge areas of walls and ceilings, is far older than the 'easel' pictures to which many of us are more accustomed. In the wide sense of the term, cave paintings from twenty thousand years ago plus are murals. The techniques that have been used throughout the progress of mural painting resolve themselves into two principal divisions; those worked on moist freshly-laid plaster, *buon fresco*, and those worked on plaster that has completely dried out, *fresco secco*. However, with *fresco secco* this dried out intonaco has to be damped before using the lime-fast colours. Slightly confusingly, there is also *secco* which means painting on the dry plaster with media such as water colour, casein, tempera or distemper without a preliminary moistening.

The term *fresco* is derived from the Italian for cool, 'fresh'. The plaster with both *buon fresco* and *fresco secco* would basically be a lime plaster mixed with fine sand and sometimes other additives that could include marble dust, but such would only be in small amounts.

As with other painting methods, the start of plaster painting is hidden somewhere deep in history. Was it the Assyrians, Egyptians, Phoenicians or Babylonians who were first to exploit this idea for decoration internally and externally? They all made considerable use of plaster for coating both brickwork and masonry.

The first mention that we have for what is apparently *buon fresco* is in the third chapter of the seventh book of Vitruvius. Pliny in his *Natural History* also mentions the technique; of interest is the fact that both the scholars assume that the method is already common knowledge and therefore it must have started earlier. Vitruvius enumerates the processes of the plastering *albaria opera* and goes on that it is provided that after the rough cast, *trullissatio*, three coats of a plaster made from lime and sand are applied, each one laid when the one below is beginning to dry. This is followed by three coats of plaster in which the sand is replaced with marble dust, at first coarse, then medium and lastly as fine as possible. He then goes on to talk of a finish with a mirror-like quality, or with stamped ornaments in relief, or with figure designs modelled by hand, or with a coat of colour which would approximate the *buon fresco* manner. Pliny uses the term *udo illinere* literally 'to paint upon the wet', *buon fresco*. The pigments with this true fresco manner are applied with no other vehicle or binder, the medium is just pure water or lime-water and the reason the colours adhere to the plaster when dry is a chemical one. One of the first concise and clear statements on this process was published in 1868 by Otto Donner von Richter. His thesis was that when limestone is burnt into lime all the carbonic acid is driven out of it. When this lime is slaked by being soaked with water it absorbs this hungrily and the resultant plaster paste becomes saturated with an aqueous solution of hydrate of lime. This paste is mixed with sand or marble dust and laid on the wall, when the hydrate of lime in solution rises to the surface, and when the wet pigment is brushed on. The colour lies on the surface, it does not sink into the plaster, and it is held there by a kind of crystalline skin of carbonate of lime – the compound that was originally voided during the burning of the lime. This crystalline skin gives a slight sheen to the surface of a *buon fresco* painting and will also give it quite a high degree of protection from an atmosphere that is free from chemical pollution – sadly, paintings can be quite easily damaged where the air carries quantities of the sulphurous fumes that belch forth in industrial areas.

Paintings carried out in *buon fresco* should always be on a wall or ceiling that is absolutely stable and free from any form of damp, as this can encourage the decay of salts in the plaster which can set off crumbling and cracking. The concussion of modern traffic, especially multi-axled multi-iron monsters, can obviously encourage cracking, also it tends to churn up a great deal of often sharp-particled dust that can do no good at all. Recently there has come even more violent concussion from the boom that top-speed jets throw out ahead of them. At least one painted baroque ceiling in a Bavarian church has been savagely cracked by this, and the author, when restoring a large mural by Niccolo Dell'Abbate (1512–1571) at a Château on the Loire, was smothered with plaster fragments dislodged by a low-flying flight of Mirages.

The history of wall painting between the Roman era and the

Renaissance is, like so much else, confused and clouded by the Dark Ages. But come the new era, the brightness of the arising genius was centred in Italy, and there the painters surged forward with a creative energy that has hardly been approached in any other period. This flow and sheer joy of achievement can perhaps be epitomised by the supreme performance by Michelangelo in the Sistine Chapel. *Buon fresco* as a medium was demanding, it required mastery from the painter, clear calculated direct expression, and in return it gave the possibility for working on a huge scale with a fluidity that allowed for freedom and effects not possible with other media.

How did the painter work? First the wall had to be meticulously prepared. A number of accounts exist in old manuscripts and although they may differ in detail, the broad scheme is the same. The wall surface to be plastered must be well scraped and hacked, the joints raked out and brushed, and the whole surface well scrubbed and wetted. The underlying layer or layers of lime and sand are then applied. The difficult part of working in *buon fresco* is that the painter has to work along with the plasterer on so-called 'day-pieces'; each 'day-piece' being the area the painter feels he can complete in one day. A 17th-century painter, Pozzo, wrote 'everyone knows that before beginning to paint it is necessary to prepare a drawing and well-studied coloured sketch, both of which are to be kept at hand in painting the fresco, so as not to have any other thought than that of the execution.' Before the final plaster layer, the *intonaco*, was laid, some painters might work out an accurate but rough sketch on the underlying plaster, called *sinopias* after the red clay that was often used in a thin wash paint for the drawing. One of the plus marks with the terrible Florence flood of 1966 was that quite a number of these *sinopias* came to light, although they had not been seen since just before they were covered bit by bit with the *intonaco*. The fresco paintings that were badly damaged by the flood waters and pollution had, in a number of cases, to be taken from the original walls and remounted. This involves what seems a horrific process to the uninitiated. The commonest method, the *strappo*, implies facing the damaged fresco with a stout canvas stuck on with an animal, water-soluble, glue; when this has hardened, the canvas is literally ripped from the bottom upwards with a strong steady pull. What happens then is that the whole paint layer comes away from the wall and sometimes exposes the *sinopia* or preparatory work. The fresco can now be remounted on a new rigid support – the adhesive that was chosen being an acrylic solution mixed with calcium carbonate. The other transfer method that the Italians are skilled with is the *distacco*. With this, first the picture surface is brushed over with a dilute acrylic fixative which will form a protective coating. After this two layers of cotton canvas are glued over the whole area with a water-soluble adhesive to which a small amount of molasses has been added to give some flexibility. When all this has dried out the canvas-covered fresco is tapped all over with rubber mallets. The whole *intonaco* layer and canvas-covered painting can be levered from the wall by using long broad flat steel knives; and the artist's original thinking on his composition comes into view. As with the *strappo*, the fresco is remounted, and after becoming quite stable the glue and cotton canvas can be removed with warm water. Now any cleaning that is necessary can take place – usually plentiful supplies of water will be sufficient, but for obstinate grime weak ammonia may be used. Often during this process of cleansing the restorers come up against strange and awful things that may have been done in the past by well-meaning but ignorant hands.

The preparation and recipe for the prized *intonaco* was a matter for considerable care. Instructions from the past speak of lime that should be prepared from a stone that is as far as possible pure carbonate of lime – Vasari, the great Renaissance commentator on Italian painters, recommended the travertine of Tivoli as perfect for the purpose. After this had been burnt it should be slaked with water and completely macerated so that there are no lumps left. The slaked lime, which would end up as a stiff paste known as 'putty', would then be covered and stored away for anything up to a year or more before it might be reckoned as ready. The proportions for mixing with the sand vary between masters, Cennini advises two parts of sand to one of 'rich' or caustic lime, the same applying to the *intonaco* for the part of the work that has to be completed that day by the painter.

The palette of colours chosen have all to be lime-resistant, and this does place on the painter quite considerable restrictions: safe colours included the earth pigments, raw or burnt, red ochre, yellow ochre, *terre verte* and a white prepared from lime. Blues present the most difficulty; azurite is attacked by lime, indigo is fugitive, and true ultramarine far too precious to be used on a large scale. Cennini advised the use of indigo and then a thin glazing with ultramarine in *secco*.

Before making a start the painter is likely to have roughed out his ideas with a *sinopia*; he will also probably have prepared a detailed cartoon as suggested by Pozzo. Once the *intonaco* has become firm enough, this cartoon can be transferred to the wall. One way is to fix it into position and then run a slightly rounded point along the main lines so that the pressure will be sufficient to make a slight impression on the damp *intonaco*, this should be sufficient to give the painter the guidance he needs. Another method is to use a roulette wheel as described on page 27.

The painter is now faced with his prepared 'day-piece' and probably stands for some minutes drawing up his courage to make a start, knowing well that a mistake can involve much costly removal of the *intonaco* and a new beginning. His assistants will have the colours all ready mixed, either in little pots on a metal palette with a rim round the edge, or on a table. It was generally the old Italian practice to have each colour mixed ready in dark, middle and light tones. The water was as pure as they could make it, by boiling or distilling it. A general custom seems to have been for the painter first to outline the figures and main details already pounced or impressed. This he would do with a long-haired brush dipped in some fairly weak red ochre. With faces he would lay in broadly the modelling under the chin, nose and brows with *terre verte*, and then blend in the flesh tones and the highlights. Hair would probably be indicated with three tones relevant to the hair colour desired. At all times the work must be as direct as possible because too much colour manipulating on any one spot can quickly destroy the essential freshness of the fresco. The brushes he used would have had longish hair or bristle heads and would have nearly always been round in shape, the hairs or bristles being from animals mentioned in chapter two. One report does mention hairs from an otter being used, but no details are offered as to the success of such brushes.

Bearing in mind the complexities of the process and the possibilities of unforeseen results, the almost incredible achievement by Michelangelo becomes even more something to wonder at. Since his boyhood he had had no practical experience with this most difficult of media. He held off the commission as long as he could, knowing in himself that he was a sculptor rather than a painter. No doubt there was much lobbying and skulduggery in the background from members of the Vatican circle who would be jealous of his genius, and other artists who might well want to see the great one trip and fall. But eventually he started. With no skilled assistants, he went to work for the most part lying on his back in a sort of cradle and painting with his arms above his head and slowly, over the months, the masterpiece grew into being.

Michelangelo triumphed. After four years, much of the time working in secrecy behind locked doors, he had divided the ceiling into great panels, joined by architectural details, single figures and groups. The subjects covered included the Creation of the World, God Creating the Luminaries, God Blessing the Earth, the Fall of Man, the Creation of Adam, the Creation of Eve, The Temptation and Fall, The Sacrifice of Noah, the Drunkenness of Noah and The Deluge. Photographs can suggest, coloured reproductions may point the way, but neither can convey the immensity of the work. It brims over with the spiritual power which Michelangelo must have felt as he poured into every figure a superb continuous sense of movement.

Since the time of the Renaissance the practice of working in *buon fresco* has largely lapsed. William Dyce and George Frederick Watts did work in it for a time in the last century. Dyce was commissioned to do a series in the Houses of Parliament but his efforts met with discouragement and, with the first examples, some failure, as they started to peel and flake soon after they were finished. To an extent he was working 'in the dark', as there was no established workshop system to aid him and he and his plasterers had more or less to learn as they went along. Since then the frescos have suffered from the vicissitudes of the London pollution and also from attempts by restorers to stabilise matters by liberally applying waxes and varnishes. Because of this, they have little of the freshness that is the beauty of this medium left.

Fresco secco, as has been mentioned, is allied to *buon* in that a similar palette would be used; differing mostly because the *intonaco* is allowed to harden before painting begins. The surface has to be well dampened before paint is applied. *Secco* painting brings in a wider variety of media that can be painted directly on to the dry, hardened *intonaco*. The plaster may not even be the specialised fine marble dust of the fresco *intonaco*, it may be quite ordinary lime plaster, and probably was in some of the early church painting in this country. The media that have been used for this manner include at least the different kinds of tempera, casein-bound colours, distemper and size paints; varying degrees of water colour and gouache could be included; types of oil technique; the so-called stereochromy; also mixtures of wax with turpentine and oils, and often some strange concocted private recipes such as the Gambier Parry Process.

Stereochromy or water glass painting is fairly close to *fresco secco* in that the adhesion of the colours to the plaster is secured by a mineral agent. The technique was not discovered till about 1825 and resulted from the work of the German chemist Von Fuchs. He found that silicate of potassium or of soda (water glass), would bind pigments to a plaster surface. The method involved using the same palette of colours as the fresco painter and applying them mixed with distilled water to the prepared plaster. By liberally soaking the dried fresco with water glass he achieved a very permanent fix. The water glass gave an almost hard, glazed finish that was little affected by the atmosphere, and could be readily washed to remove accumulated surface grime. Improvements were effected by, amongst others, Keim and Recknagel of Munich, and the method was used a good deal both internally and externally during the latter part of the 19th century. One large demonstration of the medium was by Professor Schraudolph when he used it to decorate the façade of the Hôtel Bellevue in Munich.

One recipe for the water glass medium consists of: 15 parts powdered quartz sand, 10 parts refined potash, 1 part powdered charcoal, which are all mixed together and then placed in a glass furnace and fused for between six and eight hours. The mass that emerges, when cool, is again powdered and then boiled in distilled water for up to four hours or until it dissolves. This results in a strongly alkaline syrup-like liquid which may be diluted with water and should be applied hot.

The operator having managed to prepare the above is then faced with some rigid instructions for the working of the wall surface. The wall must be thoroughly stabilised and cleaned off, and a layer of rough plaster applied. Then a layer of a special plaster, the *intonaco*, is applied; this is composed of 1 part lime to 6 parts selected fine sand and marble powder, with a small quantity of infusorial earth. The idea is to obtain a homogeneous and porous ground that will accept a thorough impregnation by the water glass solution. The *intonaco*, after it has dried out, is sprayed with an acid to dissolve the crystalline skin of lime carbonate and to further open up the plaster surface. It was found that the following colours were safe with this technique as it has developed: the umbers, siennas, ochres, Naples yellow, cobalt blue, cobalt green, French ultramarine, chrome yellow, chrome green, chrome red, *terre verte* and two whites, baryta and zinc. During the actual painting the pigments are mixed with just distilled water and, by repute, the application is fluid and simple. The painter can stop and continue days later if he wishes. When the mural is completed it is left to thoroughly dry out, then is sprayed with a hot application of the water glass; this is continued until no more can be absorbed. The idea is that the hot water glass will completely permeate not only the *intonaco* but also the underlying rough plaster and to a degree pass into the wall itself, thus binding the whole sandwich compactly together. Keim published an instruction pamphlet in 1883 which it was hoped could guide would-be painters along the right lines; the final paragraph states:

> The fixing of the picture is accomplished by means of a hot solution of potash water glass, thrown against the surface by means of a spray-producing machine in the form of a very fine spray. This fixing done, by several repetitions of the process, a solution of carbonate of ammonia is finally applied to the surface. The carbonate of potash, which is thus quickly formed, is removed by repeated washing with distilled water. Then the picture is dried by a moderate artificial heat. Finally a solution of paraffin in benzene may be used to enrich the colours and further preserve the painting from adverse influences.

The whole complicated process must have turned some painters away, although Daniel Maclise, the Irish-born artist, did use the medium for some mural work in the Houses of Parliament.

Another rather involved method was the 'Gambier Parry' technique or as it could be described 'spirit fresco', and involved the artist again in complicated work. Mr Parry waxed enthusiastic about his discovery and claimed whole-heartedly that it 'is not the mere addition of one or more mediums to the many already known, but a system, complete from the first preparation of a wall to the last touch of the artist'; he then went on to list the advantages of his method. These included permanence, as the principal materials were all but imperishable; the ability to resist external damp and changes of temperature; the retaining of a luminous effect; a freedom from all chemical action on colours; and also, rather strangely, that it had a dead surface.

His basic idea was somewhat similar to the foregoing stereochromy in that the *intonaco*, rough plaster and the wall should be so drenched with a solution that it would become a homogeneous mass. Parry, however, did not advocate a chemical mineral solution but rather a medium composed of oils, varnishes and waxes – this seems to have brought the process very close to oils. Parry further instructs that after the *intonaco* has been laid and dried out it should be well soaked with the medium that was to be prepared from:

> 4 oz pure white wax (presumably very refined and purified
> beeswax)
> 2 oz elemi resin
> 2 oz rectified turpentine
> 8 oz oil of spike (delightful smell of lavender but very expensive)
> 20 oz copal varnish

These ingredients should be melted together and boiled by a process Parry had invented (presumably out-of-doors, as the fire risk would be considerable). When used for the wall this medium was diluted with turpentine, to about one and a half of its bulk. The wall was to be well soaked with this. Further instructions follow:

> After a few days left for evaporation, mix equal quantities of pure white lead in powder and of gilder's whitening in the medium, slightly diluted with about a third of turpentine, and paint the surface thickly as a brush can lay it. This when dry, for which two or three weeks may be required, produces a perfect surface.

Apparently the surface is supposed to be both absorbent and white. This is a little hard to understand because copal has quite a deep yellow tone and it would be thought that the resins and wax would have fairly effectively sealed the surface of the *intonaco*. The pigments should be mixed with the medium and the painter told to apply them with a good deal of body and to use oil of spike as a diluent if needed. Professor Church did suggest some alterations to Parry's spirit fresco; he thought that the elemi resin and beeswax should be taken out and that paraffin wax should be added and the turpentine should be totally free of any residual resin. Knowing what can happen to a wall painting carried out with over-lavish applications of oil colours, the thought of this lot presents potential hazards to the painting and, almost certainly, problems for a conservator.

The impermanence of mural paintings is due less to the deterioration of the walls and the ceilings than to the unwise choice of materials by the painters. The medium of oils has been the cause of more trouble than most; if the application is a little too lavish and there is overmuch oil with the pigments the film will not only take a long time to dry out thoroughly but also, when it does, it will present a totally sealed skin to the atmosphere. This can cause several things to happen: any dampness in the wall will almost certainly cause blistering, in an over-dry atmosphere flaking could be encouraged, further, if varnishes were applied, cracking would be likely to ensue. Despite such matters, there have been numerous attempts in history to use oils. The main reason is that the mediums of *buon fresco* and *fresco secco* do not give the painter a rich palette with which to work; nor do the other methods of *secco* painting produce the strong power and brightness possible with oils.

In the late Renaissance time a number of artists did veer towards this medium for mural work. Leonardo used a version of it with some additives which have never really been finalised – the result, one of the world's great moments in painting, clings for life to the end wall of a church in Milan. The history of 'The Last Supper' is trouble almost all the way; even in Leonardo's time fugitive signs began to appear, and since then a regiment of restorers has fought to hold on to this treasure; some with unwise treatments, some with the best that can be devised. But today the great painting, viewed from the opposite end of the chamber, appears almost etheral, still emanating the spiritual quality of the master's conception. Its material presence is frail, but it has survived and it is to be hoped that the present comprehensive treatment will succeed at least in holding on to what is still there.

Other painters from this period tried; men such as Sebastiano del Piombo had more success. The principal factor was achieving a stable grounding on the wall; the *intonaco* of the fresco painter was not enough, something had to be added that would encourage a safe bonding of the oil bound colours to the plaster. Cennini discusses a special size for the underlayer; this should have dilute egg tempera as its base and the addition of fig milk. Another attempt at a later date was to treat the wall with several coats of hot, boiled linseed oil; someone else mixed up a brew of lime plaster with white of egg and linseed oil. None of these or the numerous other recipes have really been successful in making a plaster wall surface a happy ground for oils. Those examples that have survived are almost all thinly painted and the colours were probably diluted with turpentine. In most cases where large oil paintings have been commissioned for mural decoration, they have generally been worked on canvas which is then marouflaged to the wall using a special cement, the traditional recipe for this is white lead ground in oil.

Methods that have had success with *secco* where the *intonaco* is worked on dry – not to be confused with *fresco secco* where the

51

intonaco is moistened before the painting begins – are egg tempera (discussed in the preceding chapter), casein, distemper and water colour.

Casein can be prepared by heating skim milk and adding a little hydrochloric acid, this throws the curd out of suspension and when it is dry it is a white powder. If an alkali is added this is soluble in water and it may be used as a medium with pigments. Once the resulting paint has dried out the film will be no longer water soluble. Its main disadvantage for the painter is that the paint film can be very brittle but for mural work this does not matter. It is, however, important that the casein used is fresh stock. Today various proprietary brands of casein are available as may also be ready-mixed casein colours which have a safe washable film.

Distemper painting, as far as the artist is concerned, is a somewhat confusing term. It may imply the pigments being bound with an emulsion based on egg white and a water-soluble glue, or with one or other of a variety of sizes which could be made from hooves, rabbit skins or fish bones. Such colours are most generally used for scene painting and they will tend to have a rather flat pastel look without a great deal of depth of tone.

The use of water colour, considered by some as the most frail of mediums, for mural painting is a fairly recent departure. It is possible that earlier attempts may have been made, but they have probably either disintegrated or been painted over with other media. The principle is that the top layer of the plaster should be very carefully prepared, which could be a form of *gesso sottile*. The colours themselves would need to have some additive which makes them non-soluble once dry. The technique would make many of the same demands on the painter as would those imposed by fresco and there would be little chance of correcting a mistake or of overpainting one's way out of a difficulty. The main delight with this manner is the use and effect of the transparent colours, achieving results with layering one over the other similar to the translucence of stained glass.

The laboratory produced yet another technique for mural painting when in the late 1950s it was found that certain synthetic resins mixed with pigments would make a safe medium for the artist. These acrylic colours, as they are called, have since proved themselves as being reliable not only for wall painting but also for use with other demands of the artist. These synthetic resins had been developed in the early twenties by the American firm of Rohm and Haas, but it was not until the nineteen-thirties that they became important industrially, since when their use has become widespread. Today, in one form or another, they appear as door knobs, car tail-lights, heels for women's shoes and, to demonstrate their permanence and ability to withstand rough treatment, the white and yellow lines on the roads are prepared from them. The resulting paint film for the artist has much to commend it. Once dry little further change will occur and although tough and resistant it retains a certain elasticity which more or less precludes cracking. The basic acrylic resin medium which is the binder is a powerful adhesive in its own right and thus the colours will adhere successfully to an *intonaco* or even to a much less carefully prepared plaster surface. Indeed, if the surface of the wall to be decorated tends to be friable, the condition can be remedied by the application of two or three coats of the acrylic medium diluted with water. This allows the solution to soak into the immediate surface of the wall and to bind the loose areas into a state where it can be safe to paint. In many ways the acrylics give the painter great freedom: he may work on the wall either with the colours well diluted with water in a transparent manner, or use them quite thickly and be able to realise the textural qualities of free brushwork building up impasto. Further, the acrylic paint film when it dries can still 'breathe'. This means that even if the wall becomes damp the colours should quite safely stay in place as excess moisture can escape through into the air and thus evaporate.

Surprisingly, in English churches evidence can be found of an astonishing number of techniques either used by themselves or married together with one another. Many examples have had a rough passage, not only at the hands of amateur restorers but also from the indignity of being whitewashed over. There are little signs of the bravura of those mural masters south of the Alps, rather many of the examples left suggest almost an enlargement from the figures and details to be found in the illuminated manuscripts. Most paintings will probably date from between 1200 and 1500. Traces of different techniques that can be found include various degrees and types of fresco, some wax manners, tempera and size paintings, also gilding, glazing, raised gesso work, 'marbling' and the use of dies with metal leaves.

On the vaulting of the Chapel of Our Lady Undercroft in Canterbury Cathedral there is an interesting treatment. Suns and stars are shown in relief with small convex centres with tiny mirrors, the mirrors being made of talc backed with silver leaf. The ground of the heavens now appears as black; originally surely

53

it must have been a deep blue. What a marvellous effect could have been achieved when the small mirrors caught the light from the candles and gave an impression of celestial bodies alive with light! The pigments for the painters were probably similar to the staple ones being used in other parts of Europe – natural earths, vermilion, lime white and black – the last often being used with considerable strength to outline the figures. Time and iconoclasm have removed much from the scene, but there are still many worthwhile examples that may be visited: St Stephen's Chapel in Westminster Abbey, in particular the 'Adoration of the Magi' and the 'Presentation in the Temple'; in Canterbury Cathedral the Tester over the Tomb of the Black Prince; at Croughton, Northamptonshire, the simple rendering of the 'Massacre of the Innocents' and the 'Flight into Egypt'; the interesting remains of 'The Jesse Tree' at Weston Longville, Norfolk; the stylised Angels in Christ Church, Oxford; in Chalgrove, Oxfordshire, 'The Descent from the Cross', 'The Ascension', 'The Gathering of the Apostles' and others; at Idsworth, Hampshire, a 'Hunting Scene' and details from 'St John the Baptist'. In the Cathedral at Winchester a 12th-century painting was discovered and has proved to be one of the most exciting finds since the war. Conservation work began in 1963 in the Chapel of the Holy Sepulchre. Removal of overpainting revealed earlier paintings underneath. The paint in many instances appeared in mint condition and although there was some pitting where new plaster had been attached, the pictures were clear in every detail. During the restoration work these holes were filled in with a sandy plaster which is in harmony with the surrounding paint – the country was searched to find sand with the exact natural colouring. The artist's style is typical of the Winchester School of painters which was flourishing around 1140 and 1150 when it is felt that this work was executed. One clue is that the flowing fabrics and their treatment and the figures are related to those in the Winchester Bible. Although earlier wall paintings have been found in this country, these are certainly the finest in a church of the scale and importance of Winchester Cathedral.

The colours are brilliant, and this implies that the patrons and the artists could afford to import pigments from Europe – vermilion from Spain, true ultramarine from Italy, verdigris from France. An interesting point on the way in which influence can travel is that at Sigena in Spain there are some murals in a similar style, and it is thought likely that a monk from Winchester took the artistic tradition there.

There is one other technique for wall decoration and that is what is termed sgraffito. It is possible that the manner was first worked in Germany somewhere during the 13th century, although primitive examples could have been done sometime earlier. The peak period was during the Renaissance, and masters of the technique worked in Austria, Bohemia and Northern Italy. In simple terms sgraffito is like large-scale scraper-board work.

The artist setting out to work with sgraffito first of all has a rough plaster coat laid over the wall to be decorated and this is covered with a coat of colour; the pigment chosen must be safe with lime; this coloured layer is the ground. As soon as this ground is dry and set firm, a top layer or *intonaco* of fine plaster, perhaps with marble dust, is added, this should be smoothed down. Into this moist plaster in a manner related to *buon fresco* the artist incises his design; the cutting in has to go right through the *intonaco* and expose the ground colour. If the work is to be a large one it will be tackled with a series of 'day-pieces'; the plasterer laying just enough top coat for the artist to tackle in the day. The technique can be extended by having two or more underlayers of different colours, although this will complicate the control of working considerably.

Fragments of paintings may be found in an old building that is being restored, perhaps built over by a previous owner, or covered with colour, even plastered over or, if on wooden panels (almost the worst sin), painted over with several layers of tough old house-paint. The latter can take a lot of shifting. The techniques could include all kinds of often crude plasterwork; perhaps with a layer of lead paint as the ground, or even with the painting having been done straight into the coarse plaster, using some type of distemper, emulsion based colours, or some variant of oil colour. These fragments may be small, sometimes perhaps only details of design, portions of flowers or abstract patterning, but they are all worth preserving as they have a place in the visual history. Photograph them, but it really is best to seek skilled advice about restoration. Unskilled use of even quite mild solvents can cause havoc, whereas if properly treated often much of the original effect of the scene or fragment can be reclaimed.

If examples of any of these mural techniques are privately owned, they should be looked after as well as conditions permit, as with any other item of heritage. It is important that regular inspection is carried out, because sometimes conditions can alter unnoticed or damage can suddenly manifest itself. Visual examination needs little more than a torch and a magnifying glass to be effective. A powerful torch held at a raking angle will clearly reveal irregularities on the surface such as blistering, flaking or swellings that may be caused by moisture or mould growths. Watch for mechanical damage, abrasion caused by careless movement of furniture or other objects, efflorescence and incrustations. One common trouble in damp climates or in chambers that are below ground level is growths of algal origin, moss and possibly lichen. Depending on the importance and stability of the paintings, these disfiguring conditions can be treated with weak solutions of sodium silicofluoride or with zinc or magnesium chloride. For algae alone, formalin will often clear the disfigurement; this can be applied, taking precautions, with either a brush or a spray. If this does not work, a 2% aqueous solution of sodium pentachlorophenate may be applied with a soft brush. Mould growths and algae can often be discouraged if it is possible to increase the ventilation and to rectify stagnant areas. But allow any change of heating and humidity to be gradual; a sudden rise in temperature or a rapid drying of the atmosphere could bring on quite serious physical damage.

The Oil Painter
and His Ways

The early artists working in fresco and variations of tempera and water colour have produced pictures of often great beauty and permanence, yet in some ways they were denied a full expression for their ideas. There were limitations of palette demanded by fresco, and the tempera and water-colour methods, although they made for harmony and delicate colours, were not able to give the painter the full-blooded response he might have been seeking.

Since its inception oil painting has held pride of choice by not only artists but also their patrons. No other media can offer the painter quite so much. First in importance is the strength and richness of the colours ground with an oil, with this is coupled the many ways of application that are possible; textural effects, the 'handwriting' of the painter, when applied with hog bristle brushes; the use of painting knives to create exciting impasto effects; the sheer manoeuvrability of the paint; exploitation of transparent and opaque colours; smooth application with sables and the magic that can be uncovered by glazing clear colours over earlier applications.

The invention of oil painting as a sudden flash of inspiration has often been credited to the Flemish painter Jan van Eyck (1385–1440). Although he undoubtedly did much to improve and perfect the medium, there is evidence that others, many centuries before him, were working towards the idea of grinding pigments in oil. Oil as a vehicle releases the full brilliance of the pigments; with emulsion methods this is only seen at the moment of mixing and it fades as the paint film dries.

Pliny notes the possibility of painting with oils, he also states that the idea came to Italy during the time of Marcellus and that the Romans used such paint for decorating their shields. At the beginning of the 6th century a medical writer Aetius goes into the use of nut oil, though it is not entirely clear which kind of nut. The Lucca Manuscript of the 8th or 9th century contains a recipe for the use of linseed oil with resin. The Mount Athos Handbook shows that 'peseri', or boiled linseed oil, was regularly used, and there is also mentioned an outline for the technique of painting with oils; about 1100 Theophilus admonishes the painter to grind his pigments carefully in oil of linseed.

Oil painting is really a development from experiments made with egg tempera and other emulsion-bound techniques; painters were looking for a way to achieve brighter and stronger colours, and also for a paint that would be more adaptable to producing, for example, the rounding of forms and the full range of subtleties that the artist could observe. Jan van Eyck, who was fascinated by the showing of details, found that if he under-painted his pictures with egg tempera and then overpainted with the pigments ground with an oil and diluted possibly with tur-pentine, his aims could be attained. It is interesting, however, to note that both he and his contemporaries painted in such a way (presumably with soft hair brushes) that they effaced every trace of the brush strokes. The resulting surface bore a similarity to the flatness of tempera. Records show that experiments were also proceeding in Italy where, among others, Piero della Francesca (c. 1410/20–1492) and particularly Antonello de Messina (1430–1479) were mixing oils with egg tempera and also varnishes. In Germany the likes of Albrecht Altdorfer (c. 1480–1538), Albrecht Dürer (1471–1528) and Matthias Grünewald (c. 1460–1528) were working along similar lines.

As with some of the techniques mentioned in the earlier chapters, the progress of oil paints has been and in fact still is at times fraught with trouble, particularly so if the painter does not observe certain basic rules, or if the manufacture of the colours is not honourably carried out.

The snag with any innovation, certainly with painting and drawing methods, is that the artist concerned can only see the immediate effect and can have no advance knowledge as to what is likely to happen with the passing of time. This certainly applies very much to oils. First, what are the oils that have been used? The earliest, and the one which has been proved to be the most successful, seems to have been linseed. Others include the clear oil that can be pressed from the seeds of the opium poppy, this will give a slower drying time for the painter; and nut oil from the kernels of the common walnut. Trials have also been made with such oils as: lumbang, so-called candlenut oil from the Philip-pines; oiticica from Brazil; perilla, this one has a strong tendency to yellow with time; soya; probably sunflower; and tung which is taken from a nut from China. The desirable qualities in the oil are that it will dry naturally in the air by a process of oxidation, that this drying or hardening should not be accompanied by any undue shrinking nor by a change in colour, and that pigments mixed with it should not alter in volume or appearance during this drying process. In fact all oils, to a lesser or greater extent, will move towards a yellowing and possible darkening, although this can be minimal if care is taken. There are examples littering the history of oil painting where mistakes in preparation or the use of incorrect, poor or faulty materials have brought about dire darkening – particularly with flesh colours. The Mount Athos Handbook describes a technique of linseed oil and a gum (which could have been sandarac resin) being compounded with heat; there are hints also of other ingredients – the resulting mixture being applied to areas of flesh whilst the draperies may have been treated with wax. Such mixtures could easily bring on severe darkening. It is possible that this is the explanation for the well-known 'black Madonnas', that proliferate in Italy and the lands of the Greek church. They could be Byzantine icons painted in oils for the flesh and the draperies and other areas worked in egg tempera or other emulsion techniques.

When some of the conflicting and often weird recipes are read it seems a wonder that any number of the paintings, certainly the early oils, have survived at all. The Italian Filarete writing in about 1464 states that oil painting was especially practised in 'Germany', and that it is a fine art when anyone knows how to compass it. The medium is oil of linseed. 'But is not this very thick?' he imagines someone objecting. 'Yes, but there is a way of thinning it: I do not quite know how; but it would be stood out in a vessel and clarify itself. I understand that there is a quicker way of managing this – but let this pass, and let us go on to the method of painting.' (Probably if linseed oil was stood outside in a vessel it would be more likely to have become thicker still.)

There is a long running tragedy with the visual arts that so much of the talent poured out by the artists over the centuries has been destroyed by ignorance, ill-conceived experiment and fugitive materials and techniques – not to mention the ravages of iconoclasm, vandalism, war, fire and flood. Working in Florence after the inundation of 1966 it was grievous to witness how speedily priceless treasures can be converted into dross. However today, the most advanced techniques for conservation have to admit failure only in very few cases.

The story of oil painting as a medium in itself must start in the

15th century and thus to a high degree it is the vehicle used by most of those great masters whom a popular history of art would include. It is the medium which more than any other has been witness to the struggles and victories of the painter as he has moved forward to discover and harness perspective, light and shade, texture, colour theories, composition, and that really indescribable talent for the making of pictures. The results may be vivid portraits by Goya, imaginative moments of disaster by Danby, landscapes by Hobbema, floral bouquets by Fantin La Tour, small genres by artists such as Teniers, or the atmosphere as caught by Turner or Monet – yet all these are of the company – that band of people who have the touch to convert a few squirts of colour on a palette into something that can entrance and hold. The beauty of painting is that it is a wonderful way of communicating, and in some respects in a richer and more comprehensive way than words. Look into a picture that attracts and it is almost certain that you will come across some passage in it that 'sends you' but just why won't go into words – the enjoyment is on another plane.

What materials has the oil painter chosen to work on? In many cases it has been on a textile, generally a linen canvas. Other supports have included wooden panels, ceramic plaques, metal sheets (generally copper), slates, stones, cards, papers, glass (as with back-glass painting) and leather (there is a ceremonial parade shield of leather in the National Gallery of Art, Washington, D.C., on which is a painting of the young David by Andrea de Castagno (c. 1423–c. 1457)).

As mentioned earlier, if the oil technique is to be lasting, it does demand that the painter obeys certain disciplines. The combination of varying materials whether on a canvas or a wooden panel is a complicated sandwich.

Before the building up of this sandwich the canvas will have to be stretched. This is done on a frame of four battens of wood that have specially mitred corners that will allow the placing of small wedges; the purpose of these is to tighten the canvas when it is fixed to the stretcher; the wedges are gently tapped with a hammer going from one corner to the next to obtain an even stretch. Stretchers from the 17th, 18th and early 19th centuries had rather different fitting corners and ones that did not allow for wedges.

To make it stretch, the canvas is cut so that it is large enough to fold over the outside edges of the stretcher and brought round to the back. The general procedure is to place the canvas in position and then drive in a copper tack in the middle of one of the sides; next turn the frame and canvas round and use canvas straining pliers to pull the material taut, and drive in another copper tack (steel or iron tacks should never be used because of rusting which could rot the canvas). Repeat the process with the other two sides and then work towards one corner at a time, watching always that the tension is even and the warps and woofs are parallel with the relative sides. When this has been continued right round the stretcher, lay it face down on the bench and attach the edges to the back of the stretcher bars, folding the corners neatly into place and securing. The canvas should gently drum when tapped – it should never be so tight that it resonates. If too loose, the wedges can be adjusted; if too tight, sometimes this can be remedied by gentle taps with a mallet on the corners, or if the wedges have been driven home they can be loosened with a pair of pliers.

If the canvas is the original one, often some indication of age can be obtained by examining the tacks that the painter has used and also by the type of weave of the canvas itself. A number of the earlier ones had a distinctive herring-bone weave. Another feature is the maker's name, which may be marked with some form of stencil or stamp on the back; this applies mostly to examples from the late 18th and through the 19th century.

The raw canvas has to be first of all given a coating of animal size – this is to protect the fibres of the linen from the possible rotting effects of the oil. When this has dried out, the canvas will next be given a priming which will act as a basic ground for the painting. There have been myriad recipes for this, many so secretly guarded that the ingredients have been lost sight of.

Textiles that have been used include cotton canvases, sailcloth of varying thicknesses and surface, hessian, duck and twill; most of these are inferior to pure linen canvas with threads and warps of equal strength and weight, and they will not give a satisfactory stretch. One of the worst offenders is a linen and cotton mixture, which will have an uneven absorption and discharge of atmospheric moisture, and will be prone to distortion when stretched.

A sound priming can be made from equal quantities of lead and zinc whites, the basic vehicle being a mixture of linseed and turpentine. This should be brushed over the canvas rather sparingly for the first coat and when dry followed by a slightly more generous application. Painters sometimes mix additives such as whiting, marble dust and kaolin into their priming with the idea of producing a surface for painting that has rather more grip to it. This may be safe if the amount is only small, but if it is overdone the picture could be at risk. Various emulsion-based primers have also been used but here again there can be trouble as some of the vehicles such as egg white and some glues can make for an over-brittle layer that will crack as the canvas moves with the atmosphere. Present-day acrylic primers are safe as they have a slightly elastic quality.

After priming, the next treatment with many painters would be to lay an *imprimatura*. This is a thin veiling of colour to soften the effect of the white when painting. This thin coat of colour would be diluted with a substance similar to turpentine and applied in the manner of a wash. The colour chosen was generally one of the earths, raw or burnt umber, burnt sienna, although some painters might chose the pale cool green *terre verte* for a figure composition. If a study is made of paintings, particularly those

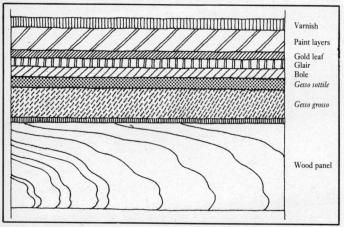

Diagram 2 Section through an oil painting on a wooden panel

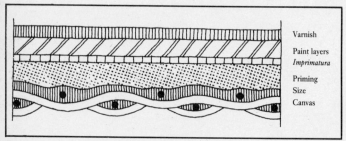

Diagram 3 Section through an oil painting on canvas

that were intended by the artist to be a sketch for a larger picture to come, vestiges of this *imprimatura* can be seen. In fact with some of Constable's and Gainsborough's work the underlying tone remains to become part of the general colour scheme.

In the early periods of oil painting it was the custom of some artists to commit their basic ideas to canvas using a thin painting of egg tempera, and later the idea was still carried on but the underpainting was applied with thin layers of oils diluted with turpentine. During this century turpentine substitute was preferred by some. The all-important rule for the painter was to follow the course taken by the house-painter which was to 'start lean, finish fat'. This means that those underpaintings must be low in oil, for if they are rich and another coat of rich colour is placed on top of them when they are only skin-dry it is likely that the two layers drying at different speeds are going to work against each other and will be liable to crack.

After the underpainting comes the final layers of colour which may be of quite considerable thickness depending upon the painter's personal style. Lastly, after a period of some months, the protective varnish will be applied. So the sandwich for an oil on canvas is going to be six decks thick. If the painter is using a wooden panel it will often be prepared with the gesso layers described in the second chapter for tempera and in this case the sandwich will be eight layers thick. If the painter gets it right, the whole will have a reasonable degree of permanence – get it wrong and many things can go awry, which will be pointed to in the next chapter.

There is another way that is favoured by artists, often depending upon the subject, and this is *alla prima*. The term implies carrying out the whole painting more or less in one sitting. The result can often have a greater sense of verve and freshness than the more laboured method, but it will call for clear visualising beforehand by the painter, as indecision will show up with the way the strokes are placed upon the canvas or panel. Treatises on painting from the 17th, 18th and early 19th centuries can be a little confusing, for the custom generally was to refer to the brush as a pencil. T. H. Fielding in his work published in 1839 discussed what would be the *alla prima* as: 'Pencilling may be divided into two kinds – viz. the bold, which is suited for despatch, requiring great knowledge of drawing, as well as the materials used in painting . . .'

This manner of brushwork is one of the most significant with the technique of oils. It is the marks that the painter makes with the hog bristle brushes as he works the colours on to the support which are all a part of his personal style and of the making of the picture with the different components – placing strokes so that they simulate textures, weaving strokes so that they give a special impression to the eye of the viewer. To explore in detail paintings from the different periods can be fascinating. From a distance of several yards the eye receives visual messages which it transfers to the mind to recognise as certain features or objects. Now move up to a canvas, perhaps by Frans Hals, keeping the eye fixed on what it has seen from the distance as an immaculately painted hand. The result, close to, shows that Hals has created the image by what might almost be called an act of legerdemain, the hand is indicated by a few strokes that give the impression of being dashed in at high speed, which they may well have been.

As the story advances, it is the tendency more and more for the artist to realise that the brush will draw as well as the charcoal or pointed pencil and what is more, that a single brushstroke put down with knowledge can draw or simulate a small object such as a leaf or petal at one movement.

The more the construction by the painter of a picture is studied, the greater can be the appreciation by the owner. Each picture is not just a matter of colours having been used but of the artist's own expression of an impression he has received. The individual treatment of trees and foliage is worth studying. Compare, for example, the broad slashing, probable knifestrokes of Maurice de Vlaminck (1876–1958) with the meticulously observed details of some of Richard Wilson's (1714–1782) early works, John Constable's (1776–1837) convincing living trees in his sketches, the foliage looking so lusciously green, an effect often achieved by the way he flicked on small touches of white, which was sneeringly derided by the envious as 'Constable's snow'. Another painter who was a great one for eye deception was Francesco Guardi (1712–1793). He had an amazing way to indicate figures; from close to they appear as a jangle of tiny spidery brushstrokes which, as one draws away, become elegant ladies and their followers by the Venetian lagoons.

One of the encouraging things for the artist from the 15th century onwards was the continual addition of new and in many ways better pigments to his palette, most of which have remained through to the present day. A recognition of these and of the choice made by the different painters can tell much about a picture, sometimes perhaps too much, as one finds that a fake

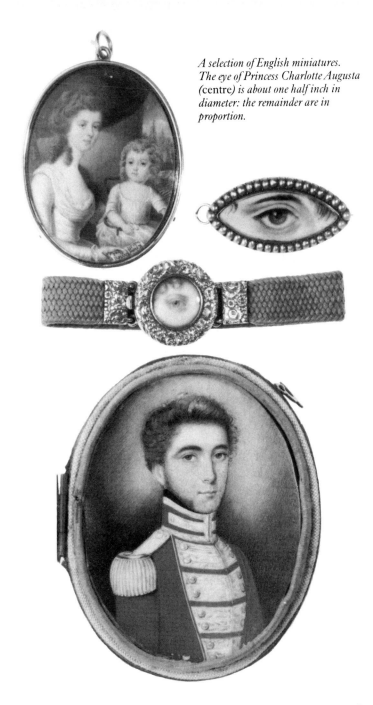

A selection of English miniatures. The eye of Princess Charlotte Augusta (centre) is about one half inch in diameter: the remainder are in proportion.

Top: River landscape attributed to William Tompkins in English giltwood frame c. 1760. Bottom: Another example of an elaborate frame. The painting is of the bridge at Shrewsbury by Paul Sandby.

18th century portrait in a frame with swept corners. Attributed to Richard Milles.

iv

Fine channelled frame with tortoiseshell surrounds a flower painting by Jan van Kessel (1626–1679).

Top left: Open carved frame, gilt, with textile covered bevelled inset. The scene shows the River Thames at Gravesend and was painted by William Anderson (1757–1837).

Bottom left: Hand carved replica of a fine Louis XVI frame.

The Long Gallery at Adare Manor, Ireland, with an example of a large double frame for portraits.

Crayon and charcoal drawing by François Boucher which has been heightened with white chalk. Such drawings should be handled with great care, since any knocking can cause the chalk to come away.

19th century chalk drawing: 'La charrette' by Jean François Millet.

Left: Chalk studies heightened with white. Top: Study of a Lion by Rubens (1577–1640). Bottom: Rural scene with sheep by Gainsborough (1727–88).

Top: Charcoal drawing, heightened with white, by Robert Healy (1768).
Bottom: Pen and ink study by Rembrandt (1606–69).

Brush drawing of a stag beetle by Albrecht Dürer. Dated, bottom left, 1505.

'Before the start', water colour and some pencil. Jack B. Yeats, 1897.

Top: 'Derwentwater', water colour by Thomas Sunderland (1744–1823).

Bottom: 'Good and Bad Angels' by William Blake (1757–1827). A coloured print finished with pen and water colour.

16th century icon of St Nicholas, on a wood panel.

Oil sketches from different periods. Top: by Gainsborough, (1727–88) on canvas. Bottom: by Vassily Kadinsky, dated 1909, on cardboard.

'Self portrait number 2', in oils, by Leon Kossof, 20th century. The painting shows very heavy impasto.

has come to light – many a forger has been stupid enough to use a pigment that is an 'anachronism, even the wily Hans van Meegeren with all his skills let his guard down and in at least one of his brilliant 'Vermeers' used traces of cobalt blue. This rather pleasant colour was not discovered until 1802 by Baron Thénard, and came into general use as an artist's colour about twenty years later. It is a compound of cobalt oxide, aluminium oxide and phosphoric acid and replaced the somewhat unsatisfactory smalt, a type of cobalt blue glass or frit, that was in demand until the introduction of artificial ultramarine.

Other pigments that have been added include:

Blues

Cerulean Blue: cobalt stannate, a compound of cobalt and tin oxides roasted together. Late 18th-century colour-makers tried to find a successful method, but the process was eventually perfected by Hopfner in 1805. It was introduced as an artist's colour in 1870 by George Rowney.

French Ultramarine: the substitute for the true ultramarine from Lapis Lazuli, was produced by Guimet in 1828.

Phthalocyanine Blue: a colour with intense tinting strength was brought into the palette in 1935. Trade names include: Monastral, Winsor, Thalo and Bocour.

Prussian Blue: ferric ferrocyanide, it was discovered by Diesbach, Berlin in 1704, and it is the first synthetic pigment with an established date. The method was kept secret until 1724 when it was published in England by John Woodward. Varieties of the colour are: Antwerp Blue, Brunswick Blue, Berlin Blue, Mothier Blue and Celestial Blue.

Greens

Emerald Green: copper aceto-arsenite, was discovered by Scheele, Sweden, in 1788, and produced commercially as a pigment by Russ and Sattler in Schweinfurt in 1814, being marketed two years later.

Hooker's Green: a mixture of gamboge and Prussian blue.

Oxide of Chromium: known since 1797 and introduced commercially as an artist's pigment in 1862.

Viridian: hydrated chromium hydroxide, it was first made by Pannetier and Binet, Paris, in 1838 as a secret product; Guignet published the process in 1859, available in England from 1862.

Yellows

Aureolin: cobalt-potassium nitrite, a strong transparent colour discovered by Fischer in Breslau in 1848, available to artists in Paris in 1852 and England about 1860.

Cadmium Yellow: sulphide of cadmium. Discovered in 1817, sold to artists in 1846. There is a range from pale yellow through to orange. For most artists the cadmiums supersede the chromes.

Chrome Yellow: lead chromate; it was originally discovered when chemists were examining a natural lead chromate, chrocoite, in the Beresof gold-mine in Siberia in 1770, and introduced as a colour in 1797. As with cadmium, there is a range of yellows through to orange. Chromes can react with other pigments.

Gallstone: prepared from gallstone of an ox, it gives a darkish yellow. Nicholas Hilliard found it useful for shading with his miniatures. John Payne in the 18th century found that dishonest colourmen were selling an inferior substitute. He suggested in his book on miniature painting that artists should approach slaughter-houses and that men there should be on the watch for gallstones. In 1804 it was one of the most expensive colours, Ackerman's showing a charge of five shillings a cake.

Gamboge: a native yellow gum from Thailand. Bright transparent golden tint valuable for glazing. It has been in use since medieval times. John Smith in *The Art of Painting in Oyl*, published in 1701, describes a method for preparing the colour, which usually comes in rough cylinders about 2½ in. in diameter.

> For a Yellow Gumboge is the best, it is sold at Druggist in Lumps, and the way to make it fit for Use, is to make a little hole with a knife in the lump, and put into the hole some Water, stir it well with a Pencil till the Water be either a faint or a deeper Yellow, as your occasion requires, then put it into a Gally-Pot, and temper up more, till you have enough for your purpose.

Indian Yellow: a now obsolete colour that was produced by heating the urine of cows that had been fed on mango leaves. It came to England in 1786, even though its method of manufacture was a mystery until the late 19th century. Owing to the cows being wasted by their diet, production was stopped in 1908 and a substitute synthetic colour was introduced.

Quercitron Yellow: obsolete colour obtained from the bark of the quercitron oak from America. It was introduced into Europe by Edward Bancroft, a Doctor of Medicine and Fellow of the Royal Society, in 1775.

Turner's Yellow: lead oxychloride. It was patented in 1781 by the English colour-maker James Turner. His recipe was plagiarised by his competitors and he nearly ruined himself with lawsuits against them. Obsolete today.

Reds

Alizarin crimson: dihydroxyanthraquinone, a derivative of anthracene, a coal-tar product. Alizarins include a red, scarlet, lake, violet and yellow. All are transparent but are slow driers with oils. Discovered in 1868 by two Germans, C. Graebe and C. Liebermann.

Cadmium Red: cadmium sulphide and cadmium selenide, introduced by De Haen in Germany in 1907, in general use in England by 1919, both light and dark shades are available.

Carmine: warm rich dyestuff extracted from cochineal insects found in Central America. Sixteenth-century artists became enamoured of it and the colour lasted through to the early 20th century. John Smith describes the laborious process:

> But at the Druggists some good Cochinele, about halfe an ounce will go a great way. Take Thirty or Forty Grains, bruise them in a Gally-Pot to fine pouder, then put to them as many Drops of the Tartar Lye as will just wet it, and make it give forth its Colour, and immediately add to it half a spoonful of Water, or more if the Colour be yet too deep, and you will have a delicate Purple Liquor, or Tincture. Then take a bit of Allum, and with a knife scrape very finely a very little of it into the Tincture, and this will take away the Purple Colour, and make it a delicate Crimson. Strain this through a fine Cloath into a clean Gally-Pot, and use it as soon as you can, for this is a Colour that always looks most Noble when soon made use of, for it will decay if it stands long.

After all that, it is fugitive and liable to fade.

Light Red: ferric oxide, calcined yellow ochre.

Browns

Asphaltum: (also termed bitumen) dark brown mixture of asphalt and oil of turpentine, sources include the Dead Sea and Trinidad. Fugitive and positively risky to use with other colours, attraction was that it made warm useful brown.

Bistre: yellow brown soot produced by charring beech wood, widely used especially with water colours between the 14th and 19th centuries.

Mummy: (also termed Egyptian brown). In the 16th century mummified bodies were imported to England from Egypt, generally being taken from the mass graves near the Pyramids. At first they were used for making internal medicines and then tried out as a pigment. The dry powdered mummy is a warm dark brown in colour and has a faint odour, rather pleasant, of spices and embalming materials. It was safer than asphaltum in an oil-glaze, and many artists in the 19th century liked it for water colour. It should be obsolete today as the export of mummies is forbidden, but some examples can still be found.

Sepia: semi-transparent brown obtained from the ink sac of the cuttlefish; it was used by the Romans but its greatest popularity was between 1780 and the end of the 19th century.

Greys

Davy's Grey: weak pigment prepared from powdered slate, it had some popularity in the late 19th century and the beginning of the 20th.

Neutral Tint: a prepared artist's colour made up from lamp black, Winsor blue and a little alizarin crimson.

Whites

Chinese White: zinc white specially prepared for water colour, introduced by Winsor and Newton in 1834.

Cremnitz White: high-quality corroded white lead made by a 19th-century method that uses litharge instead of metallic lead that is employed with the Dutch process to make flake white.

Tin White: tin oxide, first mentioned in 16th-century manuscript. Van Dyck and Mytens experimented with it and found that it blackened in sunlight.

Titanium White: titanium dioxide, properties as a pigment were known of from 1870 or earlier, not marketed until 1920. Advantage over flake white is that it is not poisonous, not so likely to be affected by atmospheric pollution and it is very opaque and mixes well with all pigments.

Zinc White: zinc oxide, first made and sold in France towards the end of 18th century, it has many of the advantages of titanium white but care is needed with some specimens as it may crack.

The foregoing list is only a fraction of the number of colours that painters have used during the past four hundred years plus; the total of all the strange pigments that have been listed by one or other of the makers would run well up in the hundreds. Today one leading maker lists one hundred and eleven pigments available as oil colours. No artist is ever going to have all those available on his painting table. Many of the greatest have indeed worked from a restricted palette; Raphael, for example, is reputed to have often used little more than four or five; these would have included yellow ochre, an umber or sienna, blue, green and a warm red. According to Busset in his book *La Technique Moderne du Tableau* the selection of colours thought necessary by Jan van Eyck was no more than eight; these consisted of genuine ultramarine, yellow ochre, orpiment, red ochre, madder, a brown earth which is not identified, *terre verte* and peach black. Study the panel of 'Jan Arnolfini and his Wife' in the National Gallery, London, or the supreme Ghent altar-piece 'The Adoration of the Lamb' in the Church of St Bavo's in Ghent, which was a joint production by Jan and his brother Hubert, and wonder at the talent that can have woven such masterpieces from such a simple palette, particularly as it contained a weak green, an unreliable yellow with orpiment and madder which can be suspect. The brothers more or less created that wonderful triptych from five pigments.

One of the greatest colourists of any time or school was undoubtedly Titian (c. 1487–1576), and by repute his pupil Giacomo Palma stated that Titian said that a fine painter needs only three colours. Another source gives Titian's palette as eight colours, but it is likely he would not have used all these together on one picture. The pigments were: genuine ultramarine, madder lake, burnt sienna, malachite, yellow ochre, red ochre, orpiment and ivory black. This remark of only three colours has much behind it, for if a painter took just ultramarine, yellow ochre and burnt umber or burnt sienna he would have the foundation for almost any type of painting, with the possible exception of a florid flower study or the portrait of a young lady or a child. The intermixes between these three are almost endless. It can be instructive to examine certain paintings close to and try to identify the colours used and to trace the mixes which the painter has made. In part this can very often help with the identification and authentication of a picture, but it is more than this. Colour is an intimate experience for the painter which is entered into by the viewer and it can be an influence for many things. Harmonies of colour, complementary colours, unusual associations of colour are very much part of the enriching and expanding of the visual experience which in its turn can lead to deeper sensations than might have been thought possible without the guiding imagery of the painter.

Most of the painters active from about the 15th century to the late 19th century seem, within certain bounds, to have kept to that basic palette mentioned previously – a good yellow, blue and brown. There have of course been many trials and errors, but in general the paint films of the early limited palettes are more stable. Part of this is no doubt due to the rigid discipline of the Guilds, and part to the fact that more attention was paid to the preparation of the support before the painting started. Some have suggested that the hand-ground pigments with a muller on a slab produced a paint with slightly coarser particles than the machine milling that was to follow and, that these coarser particles would make for a stronger film. The industrial expansion of Victoria's reign gave an impulse to the chemists, and during the last hundred years a large number of useful and exciting pigments have been added to the lists. This is reflected in the fact that many masters greatly increased the colours they used. A good example of this is André Derain; he totted up some twenty-five: cadmium yellow, yellow ochre, chrome yellow, mars yellow, strontian yellow, Venetian red, rose madder, cadmium red, carmine, vermilion, Indian red, something like a ruby madder, and another that was probably near to scarlet vermilion, saturn red, red brown, natural sienna (raw sienna), burnt sienna, ultramarine, cobalt, Prussian blue, cobalt violet, emerald green, cobalt green, ivory black and lead white. Apart from a certain degree of mental confusion which such a conglomeration might cause, it also has many pitfalls that could open up with the oils and mediums used when painting. Quite a number of the paintings by the later schools have caused, and are causing, concern for conservators. The problems can be greater because all too often it is found that the vital disciplines which can promise longevity have been neglected. Supports have been incorrectly prepared, primings have been skimped. These symptoms are examined in the following chapter.

The oil painting technique allows the artist the maximum freedom of expression: from the slightest delicate sketch with well-diluted paint on a piece of sized card or heavy rag paper, to the rugged, jagged, stabbed brushwork of Van Gogh, from the gentle subtlety of form and modelling by Jean Baptiste Chardin (1699–1779), to the bravura brushwork of Sir Peter Paul Rubens (1577–1640). The richness of pigments ground in oil gives a power and luminosity that can bring out the full quality of a portrait, yet at the same time show the softest of nuances with a frail reflected light underneath the chin, or a 'carnation' on the cheek of a young girl. Equally with oils the artist can find the gross power to portray the fierceness of the shouldering waves of the storm or the stark statement of, say, William Holman Hunt (1827–1910) with 'The Scapegoat' – the tragic animal standing in the salt crusts of the Dead Sea with the lurid sky and arid mountains in the background.

Glazing is often mentioned in connection with painting and, although it can be applied to other media, it is most of all a technique for use with oils. The explanation of the manner is simple; all it means is the application of a thin wash-like layer over previously laid colours. Thus if a painter wishes to give a more translucent touch to a red he can lay a glaze of, for example, alizarin crimson – the earlier painters would have probably used madder – over the area of the red and this can give it a look of almost stained glass. The possibilities which glazing can afford are numerous; a blue such as cobalt over-glazed with a yellow will yield a luscious green; viridian laid over a bright green will give an impression of subtle shadow, and alizarin crimson laid over burnt umber will give a wonderfully deep warm tone for interiors. The main point from the painter's angle is that the layers of paint that he intends to glaze over must be firm and dry; otherwise there is a risk of cracking and bleeding between the two applications. Another detail is that glazing can only be done with transparent colours.

Close examination can show many aspects of the way painters work which will not be obvious from several yards away. Some of the works by Canaletto (1697–1769) clearly show how he has used a careful projection to ensure the perspective is correct, some of the guide-lines are plainly visible. Return again to the ability of artists to suggest forms with brush strokes particularly in oil. Foliage is a challenge, and it is enlightening to note how painters indicate the different varieties just by the way the stroke is made, sometimes piling up the impasto with the edge of the brush to simulate broad leaves like laurel, or with downward stippled movement to give the look of pine needles of a fir against the sky. Some will have the trick of using what is quite obviously a large hog bristle to give an impression of intricate masses of foliage, others may take a small round sable or a rigger and, steadying their wrists with a mahlstick, put in place minute details. The creating of the features in a portrait can be fascinating, especially the eye and its immediate surround, and again it may be done with perhaps just three or four strokes, likewise the nose and mouth. These are not just methods of the later painters; those of the Venetian and German Schools display considerable virtuosity.

Apart from all the different kinds of brushes the painter can also make use of painting knives. These are specially made with a cranked handle, the idea being that this will keep the knuckles of the holding hand away from the paint as the stroke is made; the shapes may vary from small trowels to long-bladed ones and broad, almost heart-shaped, versions. The steel has to be of a high quality to give a very flexible touch with the paint. The knives can also be used to scratch into the wet paint or to carry out a sgraffito technique. Sometimes thin engraved lines may be seen and these are generally done with the butt end of a brush handle. If brushes and knives do not seem to give the painter what he needs, thumbs, finger tips and knuckles can be brought into play to soften an edge or scumble a thin layer of opaque colour across an earlier dried-out area, as with spray from waves or smoke from bonfires or chimneys.

One phenomenon which can be noticed occasionally is what is termed *pentimento*. This is when a thin waif-like appearance of some detail can be seen. What can have happened is that the painter has done an original lay-in for the composition, perhaps even underpainted certain parts, then changed his mind when he applied the top layers. As some oil colours dry out they can tend to become slightly transparent and thus will allow some over-strong details of earlier work to show through.

There is one other peculiarity which may be found in oils more than in other media, and this is what is called a *pastiche*. With this, a not altogether original artist will construct a composition with fragments culled from the work of others. This can be deceptive, and make the owner hope he has acquired an unsuspected masterpiece. The older the *pastiche*, the more misleading it can be. One turned up not long ago in Ireland that at first glance had an appearance of Cranach and at the second look seemed it might be by Dürer. The canvas had been relined (a conservation method described in the following chapter), but what could be seen of the original appeared to be correct for the 16th century; also the paint film had the correct look for the period; the pigments used were in line with those that either German master might have chosen. Closer examination and research eventually proved that the painter had taken one figure and part of the background from a Dürer and the other figure from a Cranach.

The position can also become complicated by copies, the making of which has been a fairly common practice through the years. In general there were two reasons; it was a method of training or it could be a commission by a patron who could not obtain the original. The trouble with copies is that they are a temptation to the 'fiddler' who can quite easily think up a provenance or add a false signature.

One slightly odd detail about oil painting is that the technique has always been a European method, spreading to America in the late 18th century, but it has never aroused much interest in the East. Although from the painted doors of the Tamamushi shrine at Nara, Japan, there is evidence that the preparation of oil colours was understood.

Oil Paintings at Risk

Although any painting, drawing or print should be treated as a fragile article, pictures painted in oils on canvas or panels, partly because of their complicated 'sandwich' construction, are prone to more maladies and physical damage than other media.

Hang and forget seems to be the practice with some owners; the pictures are brought home from the saleroom or dealers, there is a 'brief' period of admiration and then they merge into the décor and interest in them lapses. Yesterday's investment for pleasure, and possibly a future financial return, can all too easily become tomorrow's loss.

It is important to inspect the paintings on the wall at least once a year. This does not have to be an elaborate procedure. An examination with a good electric torch can pick up warning signs of cracking, blistering, flaking as well as of mould growth. Look also for buckling in the canvas, dents and bulges and marks from abrasion. If the paintings are not too large and the frames not over heavy, take them down from the wall and examine the backs. Again, watch out for mould growths, also look for signs of woodworm activity. The backs of paintings which are correctly hung with a slight cant forward, are bound to collect a fair portion of dust. This should be regularly removed because if it is allowed to collect too long it can get in between the canvas and the stretcher at the bottom and then cause bulges which are not only unsightly but also dangerous, as they will cause the various layers of the picture to crack and finally to start flaking away in the immediate vicinity of the bulges.

To remove the dust, first lay the picture face down on a stout table with a soft blanket or other material to protect the frame. Remove any securing nails or fastening strips, and lift the canvas clear of the frame. Move the frame clear of the table and replace the blanket with some smooth clean material; lay the picture face down on this. If there is any doubt about the stability of the painting, of if the canvas is weak, the safest way to remove the dust is with a flat soft-bristle brush. Always hold this with the tips of your fingers on the base of the bristles where they go into the ferrule; by doing so you obviate any danger of the metal ferrule coming in contact with the canvas, and this is even more important when the front of the picture is being dusted. With some paint films it takes only a caress with a hard object to cause quite considerable damage. Having removed the dust from the canvas, the accumulated muck that will have fallen between the canvas and the stretcher at the bottom of the picture must be cleared out. This needs care and a gentle touch, so take a plastic knife with plenty of bend in it and slide this underneath the stretcher; if you have a long-bladed painting-knife this will do even better. Now gently ease the blade along, and if there is a sudden blockage, stop. This can generally mean that a tack from the top or sides has fallen down and become wedged. With one hand, very slightly raise the stretcher when it should be possible to free the obstruction. Some might suggest using the soft brush of the vacuum cleaner if the picture appears quite sturdy, but the hand-held brush is safer and will not subject the canvas, priming and paint to vibration from the suction of the cleaner.

While the picture is out of the frame, tighten up the wedges in the corners using a small hammer. Be careful not to brush the canvas whilst striking the wedges and also do not drive them in farther than is necessary. If there is some buckling of the canvas, this may have been caused by unequal stresses on the stretchers and with reasonable care it can be adjusted by hammering the relevant wedges. Inspect the tacks, and if they have become loose or fallen out, replace with others, making sure that they are of copper. Hammering the wedges and the tacks should be done with the stretcher held vertically and adequately supported.

The siting of oil paintings on the wall should be done so that they are in no way exposed to heat sources. A favourite place is over the blazing log and coal fire. Result, tarry smoke which can come from the best-flued grates becomes deposited on the paint surface, and besides this the whole picture, stretcher and frame is subject to temperature changes, first when the fire is lit and heats up and then again in the still hours of the night when it goes out – a performance which greatly assists cracking. Where possible, avoid hot air currents from radiators or under-floor ducts, also cold draughts. Where there is central heating, any heat change should be gradual. When the heating is turned on, bring the temperature up slowly over a week, so that wood panels, stretchers and, for that matter, antiques in general, have time to acclimatise. It is not unknown for an early 16th-century painting on a panel about half an inch thick, which has seen out the centuries in its original position on the wall of some stately stone-built mansion, to be sold and then subjected to the hot dry air of an air-conditioned penthouse and, quite suddenly, split from top to bottom. The desirable mean for the relative humidity, the moisture content of the air, is between 55% and 65%. In that atmosphere, most objects of fine art and antiques will rest happily, so indeed will the inhabitants, as over-dry air does nothing for general living.

When buying a picture, particularly from an old house sale, always take a thorough look for woodworm. Often frames may be partly made from soft wood, and certainly most stretchers are, and thus they can become favourite places for the pest – in fact pictures on the move become welcome caravans for the wood-worm families and, if not detected, can easily introduce an infestation. If a wooden panel has been attacked, be hesitant about taking steps yourself. Some woodworm destroyers can contain quite strong solvents and could thus attack the paint film – it is wiser to pass the job to a professional conservator. The frames can normally be treated safely, as can the stretchers, as long as care is taken to see that the liquid does not get on the canvas. If you are having the whole house proofed against wood-worm, take the pictures off the wall and store in safety some-where. It has been known for enthusiastic operatives to include them in a deluge application with sorry results for the oil paintings.

Come the spring, watch out for the cleaner who will approach the rooms with a large bucket of water and soap and will be intent on liberally washing everything including the precious, generally unglazed, oils. Most paintings more than around fifty years old will be cracking or are cracked and thus the rich soapy suds and warm rinsing waters can get right through. Principal danger is that the size on the canvas will swell, thus lifting the priming and causing the paint film to crack, and flake. Don't fall for statements about the cleansing power of slices of potato or onion; they may clean but they will leave behind residues which can cause much trouble.

Oil paintings can have a pretty savage life unless wisdom protects them. An enormous host of would-be picture cleaners and picture 'butchers' who have picked up some fag-ends of information stand at the ready with fearsome liquids that would strip a front door in double-time. Very many oil paint films can be delicate, contain substances that are susceptible to sometimes quite mild solvents and may be a bare millimetre or so thick; they can have exquisite glazes that bring a subtle charm but which can be taken off by a clumsy swab of cleaning liquid. In no other field of conservation or cleaning can there be such a horrific risk of loss. Yet the tyros persist. A few seconds of an over-strong or incorrect solvent and they can be through the best Turner or Rubens. Some years ago I can recall answering the door to someone with an obvious picture parcel. Undoing it he exposed the remains of what could have been a pleasant 18th-century portrait; the trouble was that where the face should have been the bare canvas was showing through. This, he explained, was because in his efforts to get it clean he had rubbed pretty hard – with *what* – with a well-known bath scouring powder! That account is true, as sadly are many others of the ghastly things that have been done to the poor defenceless canvases. The conservation of works of art is something that in nearly every case should be left strictly to the trained conservator, and this applies to pictures most of all.

Restoration of paintings has been going on for centuries, sometimes even during the life of the artist, and many of the recipes to be found in old books have been hazardous. In fact, if the dangers of ignorant restoration are added to vandalism, careless handling, fire, flood and other risks, it is rather wonderful that we still have with us so many treasures – even if some of them have been 'skinned' and rubbed about until they hang pale, grey and withered in their frames. There was a hard-working amateur restorer who practised in Rome who was wont to boast that there were no secrets about picture-cleaning and advocated solvents made up of such ingredients as turpentine, spirits of wine (another name for alcohol) and potash water or soap. A dealer who thought that a caustic soap would do wonders might possibly get away with it if he quickly slapped on a coat of tinted varnish, and then sold the result to someone the other end of the kingdom.

The trouble is that an oil painting not under glass will inevitably become dirty because of muck and smoke in the atmosphere. But all the darkness on a particular picture will not be dirt. A large part may be darkened varnish. Until about thirty years ago the varnishes available to the artist were prepared from natural resins such as copal, damar, mastic, sandarac and others. All varnishes made from these will tend to yellow and darken;

damar the least and copal the most. These varnishes are also prone to crack, as the films when dried can become very brittle. One concocted during the 18th century with egg white and copal ended up with a film that is nearly bullet-proof and will respond to very few solvents. This darkening of the varnish coat can become quite intense, so much so that it is nearly impossible to see the picture at all. Certainly during the last century the 'old master look' became almost the accepted thing, and often this was compounded by dealers who would add yet another coat of varnish or, if the picture had been cleaned, would apply a good thick copal with an added darkening tint.

This fashion of revarnishing cleaned paintings with warm tinted varnishes sadly extended well into this century. It does, of course, hold an advantage for the rogue restorer, that if he has taken matters a little too deep or has had to resort to too much retouching, it will help conceal the errors. It is possible to find paintings that were cleaned just before the last war which have been treated in this way and sometimes worse. The colouring matter can be bitumen which does produce a comforting glow and superficially gives the poor painting a rich look. One set of paintings treated in this way must have had three or four coats of this brown treacle brushed on them; the result was that if a solvent was applied the whole surface became a syrupy sticky mess.

What are the aesthetics of cleaning and conserving a picture and, for that matter, ethics as well? Surely to re-establish the optical effect to something approaching that which it had when it left the artist's studio and to stabilise its construction to prolong its life. Often the shock of having a cleaned painting returned to him sends the owner close to the edge of hysteria, so accustomed may he have become to the dark, yellow brown rectangle that has hung in the dining-room for generations. He may then turn to the conservator and say bluntly that he liked it better when it was dirty, it was more harmonious and fitted in with the dark oak furniture and panelling. One instance nearly provoked an awkward moment – a family portrait by Gainsborough showed a browny-grey haired lady in a darkish green costume. After most careful treatment the conservator took back a delightful Gainsborough portrait of a beautiful blonde-haired young lady in a blue costume. Surprise from the owner, but joyfully, after having the painting back on the wall for a couple of weeks, he rang the studio to say how wonderful it looked now it had settled down.

Some books on conservation still quote solvent recipes which can in many cases be lethal to an oil painting, others are listed that in skilled hands would be safe but in untrained hands could very quickly cause damage. Knowing what may be used is one thing, applying them is quite different – after all everyone knows the kind of scalpel a surgeon uses but fortunately they don't all have a go!

One such process that is advocated states that a start should be made using a mixture of soft soap and warm water with a small amount of ammonia added – this would be excellent to clean the interior paintwork of the house but for Constable and Co., no!

The instructions are to follow this with a mixture of ammonia, methylated spirit and turpentine. This could, in a few instances, possibly be reasonably safe in the hand of an expert, but it could equally well go through some varnishes and paintings too with considerable speed. It will never be known how many would-be picture restorers have picked up information like this and how many canvases have been mortally wounded.

The only safe cleansing that can be attempted is to use a substance such as Winton Picture Cleaner to lift off surface grime, sooty deposits and much nicotine, but will not remove varnish nor, if the instructions with the bottle are followed, will it harm the painting if it is more than around thirty years old. Before using the cleaner the canvas should be supported. If cleaning on the flat a block of wood or something like chip board should be cut to fit inside the stretcher and be the same thickness as the stretcher bars; cover this with a protective film, Melinex is the one favoured by conservators, and place it into position. If the cleaning is going to be done vertically with the painting clamped on an easel, cut pieces of cardboard that will fit between the stretcher bars and the canvas. This prevents damage to the paint surface when the cleaning reaches the area over the edge of the stretchers. Always before starting make a small test at the edge underneath where the rabbet of the frame will go.

Do not attempt to clean too large an area at once, first try a couple of square inches; have the cleaner on a piece of cotton wool in the right hand and another piece of cotton wool soaked in white spirit (turpentine substitute) in the left hand. Keep examining the cleaning swab to see if by any chance colour is coming away or if loose flakes of colour are being picked up. If either of these things happens, stop at once.

There is one kind of painting that should never be touched except by a trained hand and that is one that has bitumen in its general make-up. The condition can be recognised all too easily

– the surface will have a craquelure that at times can resemble the skin of an alligator. More than this, some of the pigments can be seriously discoloured and the painter's brave intentions are brought low and the life of the picture is sullied. Just who was the first artist to introduce bitumen (or asphaltum as it is also called) is not known, but certainly the first painter of prominence to employ this deceitful and fugitive pigment was Sir Joshua Reynolds. He was a great experimenter, and was wont to try all kinds of devices to achieve the end he sought. He fell victim to the warm, entrancing deep brown of bitumen, using it liberally in so many of his fine portraits. At first he must have thrilled to the ephemeral beauty the pigment conjured on to the face of his canvases. But, by the time the colours had dried out, many were stained and discoloured and the surface reduced to a foul texture. A Reynolds having a liberal dose of bitumen is one of the nastiest problems the conservator can face because, almost as soon as any solvent touches the surface, the wretched bitumen comes alive and, in the ensuing mess, it is very difficult to see just what is happening.

William Blake, an artist who may have used some strange methods himself, had a real passion for taunting and insulting poor Joshua Reynolds, who was on the account of several people a kindly man. Blake liked to make comments on the Discourses which Reynolds gave annually to the students of the Royal Academy, of which he was President. One vilifying passage ran:

> Having spent the Vigour of my Youth & Genius under the Opression of Sir Joshua & his Gang of Cunning Knaves Without Employment & as much as could possibly be Without Bread, The Reader must Expect to Read in all my Remarks on these Books Nothing but Indignation & Resentment. While Sir Joshua was rolling in Riches, Barry was Poor & Unemploy'd except by his own Energy; Mortimer was call'd a Madman, & only Portrait Painting applauded & rewarded by the Rich & Great. Reynolds & Gainsborough Blotted & Blurred one against the other & Divided all the English World between them. Fuseli, Indignant, almost hid himself. I am hid.

The gadfly jabs go on. On Reynolds' death in 1792 Blake wrote:

> When Sir Joshua Reynolds died
> All Nature was degraded;
> The King drop'd a tear into the Queen's ear
> And all his Pictures Faded.

Unfortunately Reynolds started a fashion and a number of talented artists used bitumen because it promised them great depth in the shadows; but the result was always the same – to a lesser or larger extent – this horrid rough skin would appear; even when the wretched stuff was used only as a fine glaze the painting would not be safe.

Another disfigurement that can arise is what is termed 'bloom'. It appears as an unsightly misty cloud rather like the bloom that appears on the skins of black grapes – it is generally more evident over areas that have a preponderance of dark earth colours. No one is completely certain what is the exact cause, but the onset is connected with damp and a chilling of the atmosphere. Generally it is simple to remove. Often a dry piece of cotton wool will do the trick, or a slight buffing with a silk rag. If more obstinate it can be treated with a high quality picture wax varnish. Some advocate a drop of linseed and a drop of turpentine mixed and rubbed on with a piece of cotton wool and then well rubbed off afterwards. It is possible a painting may be discovered that is bloomed all over – this is best dealt with by cautious use of picture wax varnish. Before doing any of these treatments, be quite sure that the paint film is stable and the canvas sound. It is possible, although rare, that a bloom condition may be under the varnish and this will entail a varnish strip by a professional. Bloom is almost entirely a condition that affects natural resin varnishes. The modern synthetics are unlikely to be affected.

In the damper areas of the country and especially in some old and rather damp houses, mould growths may attack a painting either at the back of the canvas or sometimes coming through to the front. The wisest course is to move the painting to a place in which it can really dry out and then take the picture out of doors and, with a soft-hair brush, gently disperse the dry remains. A very light spray of thymol as a saturated solution in alcohol on the back will discourage a further onslaught. If a more severe attack is discovered, not only on the canvas but also the stretchers and frame, pass the problem on to the trained hand.

An oil on a canvas, especially one that is ageing, is a delicate thing and can easily be dented either from the front or the back. A common cause of damage from the front can be an ornament carelessly left touching the canvas; denting from the back may be caused by objects falling down behind or by bundles of wire from a picture light. Depending on the value of the painting and the size of the dent it can be possible to rectify this quite simply.

Remove the picture from the frame and lay it face-down. Dip a piece of cotton wool in clean water then squeeze it out and very gently rub it with a circular motion over and round the damage on the back of the canvas. It is important that the minimum amount of moisture is used and that there is no sign of damage to the paint. Leave it to dry naturally and do not apply any heat.

There are two other things to avoid with regard to the back of the canvas. Never stick labels with details about painter, subject, etcetera on the actual canvas; many adhesives when they dry can have a considerable traction and can distort the canvas; stick any labels on to the stretcher. The second matter is concerned with security devices such as the small trembler gadgets. These can be excellent but should never be stuck on to the canvas because the synthetic glues that may be used can penetrate through and upset the priming and paint layers; again fix to the stretcher.

With regard to the back of the canvas, it can be a good idea to give it some form of substantial protection. A piece of hardboard will serve well. Cut this so that it may be fixed to the stretcher and drill a few small holes at the top and the bottom to allow for ventilation; fix in place with screws (not nails) to allow for easy removal.

Among the more serious damage that can happen to a painting on canvas is a tear – very easily done, a sharp corner of a heedlessly carried tray, a high-backed chair thrust back against a wall – it should be attended to as soon as possible. Most tears take the rough form of a 'T' or an 'L' which gives them a tendency for the corners to curl, and if this happens the priming and paint layers are going to crack and there will inevitably be some paint losses. If a conservator cannot be reached fairly soon it is wise to make a temporary repair. Place the canvas face down on a stable support with a protecting layer of smooth paper or plastic sheeting. Make the repair with a tape about an inch wide which has a non water-soluble adhesive. If the tear is small it should flatten out quite simply with a finger tip and then the tape can be pressed into position. If the rent is a large one, try flattening it out with the weight of a book or books holding the rip in place and then start laying small strips of the tape, watching all the time that there is no buckling. One thing you must never do is put any sticky tape on to the front of a picture. Don't be tempted to put on a more permanent patch yourself because the professional way to treat the damage is to apply suitable material, generally some soft cotton or thin linen (never thick canvas, as it will inevitably show from the front), and this material will be held in place with a thermo-plastic adhesive made from beeswax and damar resin. The two are melted together in a double container and when thoroughly blended are applied to the torn canvas and the patching material, and then, using a special iron or electric spatula, the patch is secured in place. A piece of heat resistant plastic is placed over the patch and a cold iron is left over the area because quick chilling is necessary for the wax-resin mixture to adhere properly.

Sometimes if the tear is very large and the canvas frail, the advice from the conservator will be that a relining is needed which means placing the whole picture canvas on to a new canvas. This course may be called for if the canvas is of such an age that it is in danger of coming away from the stretcher and has deteriorated. The relining process is quite a normal happening: in fact most canvases as they approach their centenary will require to have this done. In brief, this is what happens: the picture is 'faced' with tissue and a water-soluble adhesive or special plastic sheet and is then cut from the old stretcher; a large piece of new canvas is cut to give room for fixing to a new stretcher; this is then stuck on to the back of the old canvas with either a water-soluble glue adhesive – the method favoured for a long time – or with the more modern way of the wax-resin mentioned above. Heat is applied by an iron or the whole attachment process can be done on a hot vacuum table. Lastly the new canvas with the old picture in place is stretched on to the new stretcher.

The more desperate course which has to be taken at times if the canvas and ground have rotted or if the wooden panel has decayed, is what is termed a 'transfer'. This time-consuming and hazardous process means that first of all the painting, whether on canvas or wood, has to be substantially 'faced'. If on canvas, this is removed, thread by thread, from the back. If on wood, the panel has to be lifted with infinite care, shaved, and picked away, then sometimes the ground, if of a gesso base, has to be taken off. This latter calls for magnification and the meticulous use of scalpels. (One small panel in post-flood Florence could take weeks of agonising effort until finally one was left with just the paint layer; if tempera, a highly sensitive micrometer was needed to measure the thickness of the film.) The paint layer is of course seen from the back. The ground has to be renewed and then the practice is to put the picture on to fresh canvas whether or not it was on a wood panel before.

If a wooden panel is cracking, it should really have attention as soon as possible or it may split into several pieces. Depending on the value or rarity of the panel, remedial action can be taken and this should consist of sticking small flat pieces of hardwood down the line of the cracks; the adhesive used may be water soluble such as Scotch or rabbit skin glue. Leave the patches or 'buttons' as they are termed to set with a weight holding them down for twenty-four hours. For a severely cracked panel or one that has already split apart the services of the conservator will definitely be needed. A system of consolidation with special woods and waxes will be called for, and this needs a good deal of experience.

Reference has already been made to the conditions of flaking and blistering. What this implies is that the paint layer has been forced up by some irregularity with the ground or sizing. This can be caused by damp or, on the other hand, it can be brought about by excessive dryness which has made the whole painting sandwich desiccate and lose cohesion, the various layers starting to laminate. This again is strictly for the professional, the areas will have to be carefully relaid using a heated electric spatula and the wax-resin adhesive.

How does the paint layer behave itself with the passing of time? A painting in oils starts to 'age' as soon as the artist has finished it. The materials he has used go through a drying process which can set up internal stresses in the sandwich. Depending on the thickness of the paint this can go on for years, with impasto like Van Gogh's or some of the more explosive action painters the time could stretch to twenty years or more. In the beginning as the paint film dries it absorbs oxygen from the air which can increase the bulk and the weight of the upper layers. A gradual loss in weight follows the initial increase and then shrinkage can make the paint layers move and cracks are formed. If the painter has done his preparatory work correctly and used stable materials the painting will not suffer visually from these changes. The small cracks may garner dirt but they can be cleaned out. More serious cracks which are caused by tensions in the paint can be visible to a greater extent; these are termed 'drying cracks'. One cause can be the action of two layers of colour drying out and exerting contra-tensions; with this the top layer may move quite considerably and expose the under layer. Zinc white can be the offender or it may be the addition of too much oil when painting or a badly-prepared ground.

Treatment will have to be by a conservator, for it will call for real expertise. Retouching requires great patience to ensure that it does not go over and cover any of the original paint. Pass down a dealer's row with windows showing enticing examples of old master works. Look close, and if there is no sign of cracking it is a miracle or a gross case of over-painting. An immaculate appearance is quite false, because these works from the studios of the past just must be cracked – the lack of it should arouse suspicion.

A little observation should soon train the eye to pick up the difference between paint cracks and varnish cracks. The latter will of course disappear when the picture is cleaned and the varnish is removed. Fakers and forgers are generally expert at manufacturing cracks either with the paint film or with the varnish. Paint films can be most convincingly cracked by mixing the dry pigments with egg white and, after they have been painted on, using a hair dryer on the surface. In a matter of minutes some fine cracks will be formed. Varnish will respond to 'fiddling'. While the varnish layer is still tacky it is brushed over with a fairly thick Scotch glue; as the two harden out they will set at different speeds and form a splendid and quite convincing pattern of cracks.

The surface of the paint can often disclose much about the story of what has happened to the picture over the years. Play an ultra-violet lamp on it and more information may appear. The rays of the lamp are liable to cause retouches done in the not-too-distant past to fluoresce and show exactly where damage has been made good. An infra-red photograph can show up much of the artist's underworking by penetrating the layers. Retouching can be the curse of collectors, for a clever operator can do much to disguise faults, also it may be found that changes have been made to conform with fashion, personal prejudice and political and ecclesiastical directives. Many an over-exposed lady has had her dress adjusted or an extra long lock of hair judiciously draped to calm the flutters of a prude. Flags and ensigns have been altered, adjustments made to uniforms and decorations. In one case the portrait of a university don was being treated and it was found that there was much overpaint. First the college ceremonial hat came off this gentleman, then his gown and finally a rather bushy beard. Underneath all this was a charming Dutch portrait of a man with a black skull-cap and a small goatee, down in the bottom right-hand corner was the signature 'Nicholas Maes'. The reason for such seeming nonsense can be difficult to find out.

One slight menace with pictures can be a house-fly who will

leave his small pointillist offerings across a painting, often favouring the sky. Take a cotton bud and lightly damp with water and very gently stroke the spot; if it resists, try another bud with white spirit. If this too fails, be wary about taking more drastic action because this nuisance can sometimes be quite firmly seated. If doubtful, ask for advice.

After using the Winton Cleaner referred to earlier the oil will benefit from a fresh coat of varnish. Present-day synthetic varnishes are reliable, water clear, bloom resistant and are not likely to crack, as they have a plasticiser in their make-up, and they are unlikely to darken with time. If you have a recently painted picture, be sure that it is at least twelve months old before it is varnished.

If convenient, choose a warm dry day to apply the varnish; pour a little out into a saucer and with a wide hog bristle brush give the painting a thin, even coat. Have the picture placed so that it can be seen if there are any runs of excess varnish. Apply the varnish with short criss-cross strokes and be sure that no areas are missed. The picture may be vertical on an easel or flat on a table. When finished, leave to dry in as dust-free an atmosphere as possible. Picture varnish may be bought in aerosol cans but it will need some practice with these to get an even film. There are also picture wax polishes which can give a low sheen or matt finish.

Paintings in many ways say much more to us than other antiques, for besides being aesthetically pleasing many of them carry recordings from the time they were painted, not only just costume and looks but information about the way life was lived. Small or large, precious or not so rare, most will have something to pass on. In that sense whose are they? Perhaps they are a silent comment for all from any time. Look after them, they are worth it.

Miniatures and
Ways with Glass

The work of the medieval illuminators must have been one of the inspirations for the English School of miniature painters; the name itself being derived from minium, the strong but dangerous red used by the early scribes. Many would credit Hans Holbein the Younger (1497–1543) for being the one who, more than others, brought the art off the pages of illuminated manuscripts and to the notice of the court and its followers. Holbein visited England for the second time in 1531; and started to paint a series of portraits in opaque water colour on small circular pieces of vellum. Today there are acknowledged to be only about twelve of these tiny masterpieces still existing; amongst these are the portraits of Anne of Cleeves and Mrs Pemberton that are in the Victoria and Albert Museum. The talented German painter brought a star quality to these little paintings, giving them a sense of stature beside his other works; they combine a sensitivity of draughtsmanship with strong exquisite colour and a perceptive reading of the character of his sitters.

Miniatures were painted on a number of supports including: thin sheets of ivory, vellum, chicken skin, cards and a small number were on small sheets of copper, ceramic plaques and examples may be found on leather and other materials. Generally water colours, with some body substance added, were used. Other media used include egg tempera, other temperas and well-diluted oils. The brushes are always from hair and those from the finest sable would be selected. The size would be from o, oo, or ooo – the last is termed a triple goose and has a point almost as sharp as a needle. The ivory sheets need careful preparation, as first the surface must be thoroughly smoothed over. The drawing for the portrait would be transferred, and then the lines washed over so as to leave the merest signs of them – so faint that they would not be in evidence when the painting was finished. Then the ivory would be given some form of priming; one recipe for this was a thin solution of glycerine and gum arabic which would tend to enrich the colours and increase their permanence. Some workers might apply a form of *imprimatura* such as vermilion to the reverse side of the ivory sheet, the idea being that this would shine through the milky opacity of the ivory and give a general feeling of warmth to the colours used. The colours were placed on the ivory with a form of dry stippling as tiny dots or dashes, the painter would often have to resort to a magnifying glass. The vogue for miniature painting lasted from Holbein's time until about the middle of the 19th century. These little jewel-like portraits might be displayed in intricate frames of craftsmanship to match their quality; but often as not they were intended to be portable; memories of loved ones that could go travelling with their sweethearts as they journeyed far and wide. It may be coincidence that the miniature as an important art form faded away when it did, coinciding with the invention of the camera.

The English-born painter who must be given the credit as the founder of the native school was Nicholas Hilliard (1547–1619). He was born at Exeter, the younger son of Richard Hilliard who served as High Sheriff for the county of Devon in 1560. The young man was brought up in the workshop of a goldsmith and jeweller and soon showed his talent for painting in miniature. His works were painted not on ivory but on card or chicken skin, and sometimes even on the back of playing cards. Inspired by Holbein, he was appointed goldsmith, carver and portrait painter to Queen Elizabeth I and painted her several times; later he received similar appointments with James I. His smallest works could fit into a ring and they all have a perfection of quality that is hard to credit, especially when viewed under a glass. It almost seems as though each thread of a lace collar is visible, each hair on the head and the jewellery of both ladies and gentlemen appear to have a third dimension.

Hilliard in his own time raised miniature painting to a high standard challenging the position of the conventional portrait painter. He was famous for his perfection and from then until today his works have been highly prized by collectors. John Donne the celebrated poet wrote of them:

> And a hand, or eye
> By *Hilliard* drawne, is worth an history
> By a worse painter made

Keeping to the high performance came Isaac Oliver (c. 1556–

1617), a pupil of Hilliard's. He added to the lessons of his master with at times a gentle sensitivity that probed deeper into the character of his sitters. The tradition was carried forward by Peter Oliver (c. 1596–1647), the eldest son of Isaac, probably by his first wife. He studied with his father, and is noted for the richer colour he introduced and also his exquisite handling of faces and hands. Charles I was a patron and amongst other commissions he gave Peter Oliver the task of making miniature copies in water colour of many of the finest paintings in his collection, works by Correggio, Holbein, Raphael, Titian and others. These tiny masterworks were put in small frames which had locks and were shown in the inventories as 'shutting glasses'. Charles liked to take them with him on his travels so that he could enjoy the beauty of his collection. Sadly they were dispersed with the sale of the royal pictures, although a few may still be seen in the Royal Collection at Windsor. Apparently a great many of Peter Oliver's miniatures remained in the possession of his widow and it is said that Charles II heard of this. He went privately to see Mrs Oliver accompanied by a man who was employed by the king for somewhat spurious duties. The lady showed Charles a large number of finished and unfinished miniatures. The king took away those that pleased him and later sent a message that she might have a thousand pounds for them or, if she preferred, £300 a year for life. Mrs Oliver chose the latter, but unwisely she gossiped about the monarch and his mistresses and her words came to the royal ear. Her annuity was promptly stopped!

Another talent of the English School was John Hoskins (c. 1600–1644), of whom Graham's 'English School' says:

> he was bred a face painter in oil, but afterwards taking to miniature, far exceeded what he did before; that he drew King Charles, his Queen, and most of the court, and had two considerable disciples, Alexander and Samuel Cooper, the latter of whom became much the more eminent limner.

Those who chose copper as the support for their painting often worked with enamels which demanded much from the artist, the technique is far more complicated than water colour and there are many possibilities for failure. The design has to be pencilled in and once done cannot be altered. But if successful the beautiful translucent colours gleam as jewels; some masters even used small sheets of gold and silver to work on. One of the most accomplished artists with miniature enamels was Jean Petitot

(1607–1691). He was born in Geneva, the son of a sculptor and architect. Jean came under the patronage of both Louis XIV and Charles I. He was joined by Pierre Bordier and they worked together, with Jean painting the faces and the hands and Pierre painting the draperies and backgrounds. The two artists were shown some advanced methods for enamelling by Sir Theodore Turquet de Mayerne who was physician to Charles I.

Miniature work in the 18th century in Britain was largely dominated by Richard Cosway (1740–1821), another man from Devon, being born at Tiverton where his father was master at the public school. His studies included a period with Hudson, who also numbered Reynolds amongst his pupils, and then Cosway attended the St Martin's Lane School and the Royal Academy. After, until he could fully support himself from his art, he taught in Parr's Drawing School. In haste to succeed as a free-lance he took on much work, with some of which he allowed his discretion to become blurred; there were examples of not so chaste glimpses of fair ladies for the snuff boxes of the rakes around town. Such lapses gave fuel to the jealous ones who spread stories of charlatanism and worse about a man who had great talent. Cosway was a strange character, small in stature, mean in purse, yet vain for his appearance, and his studio was filled with luxurious objects. His wife, Maria, born in 1759, was the daughter of a hotel-keeper in Florence and she also painted portraits 'in little'. Maria was a talented musician and did much to further her husband's career.

In his manner of work Cosway produced considerable subtlety with miniatures on ivory; he tended to discard the opaque manner and to adopt an approach of great delicacy. His minute strokes had a silvery nuance about them and captured a sparkling charm from the sartorial fashions of his sitters; the décolleté bodice, the frilled chemisette, the powdered and sometimes outrageous hair styles. More than most, Cosway impinged his character into the miniatures rather than the likeness of his sitters. He has been criticised for his facile compositions and the small conceits he sometimes employed, but, when it comes to the purely technical, Cosway in his time had no peer.

He is credited with the introduction of a rather off-beat vogue and this was the painting of just one eye of the sitter in miniature. The ball was set rolling when Mrs Fitzherbert commissioned him to paint her right eye as a gift for the Prince Regent, who promptly responded by having one of his eyes painted and then set in a ring which he gave to Mrs Fitzherbert as a birthday gift.

But after a short time it seems that eye-painting palled on Cosway and he left one of his rivals, George Engleheart, to make the running, and this artist probably painted more eyes than anyone else, especially in the early years of the 19th century. For one family he painted a whole series, and his studio note-book for 1804 contains the following reference:

Captain R. Beauchamp, his eye.
Captain R. Beauchamp, his left eye.
Mr. Richard Beauchamp, his eye.
Mr Thomas Beauchamp, his eye.
Lady Beauchamp, her eye.
Sir Thomas Beauchamp, his eye.

Others who made a point of painting eyes at this period were Sir William Ross and Anthony Stewart and possibly Ozias Humphrey, but the work of the first two did not approach the standards of Engleheart who seemed to be able to impart a clear and liquid reality to his tiny pictures. The fashion appears to have lost popularity after Stewart and Ross. There was the somewhat dramatic painting of the eye of Lady Holland which was made by George Frederick Watts (1817–1904), this was made larger than life-size and was set in a mantelpiece at Holland House. It possessed a weird reality and seemed to watch and follow any visitor to the room. Apparently Lady Holland's eyes differed considerably in colour and size; Watts must have painted his version soon after Lady Holland returned from a trip to Italy where she probably saw a representation of an eye painted in the centre of the cupola of a church in Rome. There are several places in Italy where a large eye, intended to represent the vision of the Almighty, looks down on the worshippers. There was reputedly an example of such Italian workmanship in a Gloucestershire house; a large eye in the point of a dome gazed down on all those who entered the hall.

The larger of the eye paintings were transgressions from the true miniatures which in dimensions were limited, if painted on ivory, to the size of the tusks – although there were attempts to join the small sheets together invisibly this was not very successful. Thus a miniature would be a maximum of around seven by five inches.

For some, undoubtedly the great period of the miniaturist was from the latter part of the 16th century to just after the middle of the 17th century. Although talented technically, the work of Cosway and his followers has a sensation of the ephemeral when placed beside those of Hilliard and Cooper. The earlier masters worked with a direct truth and simplicity not aided by artifice or affectation. It could be that this is another instance of those great peaks that come in the visual arts. Sometimes these are dominated by a group of people and at others just by a single person. The light of inspiration leaps up almost as unpredictably as 'will-o'-the-wisp', both in time and geographically. A glance at the history of fine art and antiques underlines this. The time of the Renaissance must be high in precedence with a flowering of genius right across the scene; from there the rays of inspiration set up following centres through the years. The progress of art should not be seen as a series of stops and starts but rather as a continuous process that moves to an environment and an atmosphere that encourage it.

There have been instances where techniques with painting and with crafts have been invented or developed by artists and then have disappeared, or the skills for them have not been forthcoming. In the first chapter various methods that were used in Egypt, Greece and Italy were discussed, although even today the experts are not quite sure exactly what the materials were that had been used. In the National Museum of Ireland in Dublin there are some fine objects of gold smithed by the early Celts; amongst these is a slender cord of gold thread, apparently made by some form of crochet or intricate plaiting. The gold thread is almost hair-thin, but how the ancient craftsman did it is still uncertain.

Many artists in their search for a perfect way of expression have sometimes hit upon a substance to mix with their pigments that will give a release for the method they seek; it is not absolutely certain what Rubens used to achieve his long sweeping strokes or what was the process in detail employed by the Pompeiian wall painters. At times artists seemed bent on challenging some extraordinary difficulties with techniques that might appear to be unsuitable for the task in hand.

One of the most basically simple but at the same time most subtle and refined techniques that has ever been used for pictorial expression is a method that is today termed *verre églomisé*. This term was derived from an 18th-century dealer, Jean Baptiste Glomy, who died in France in 1786. Glomy was apparently also a picture framer who started a fashion of surrounding a subject with a border of gilding and colour painted behind glass. Prints framed in this manner became known to the trade as 'églomisées'. In 1852 the term took on some respectability when it appeared in a catalogue of the Musée de Cluny; the Italian version being 'agglomizzato' – the terms being loosely applied to any form of gilding and painting behind glass of any date.

Actually work in this manner goes far back in history. The practice of engraving through gold leaf and sometimes other metallic leaves is first noticed with the Romans, especially the later Roman period and the Early Christian time. There were some fine examples made in Italy during the early Renaissance and then, in the early part of the 18th century, came an upsurge of popularity centred apparently round a Bohemian monastery.

The method of working has something in common with dry-point and also with painting. The first step is to take a sheet of sound and flawless glass, which should be much easier today than it was some hundreds of years ago. The surface of the glass should then be thoroughly de-greased, wiped and dusted absolutely clean. The adhesive for laying the gold leaf or other metallic leaves may be one of several. Many of the early masters stuck faithfully by glair, that mixture of very well-beaten egg white and pure water. The gold leaf selected should be somewhat heavier than normal and it must be laid absolutely flat on the glass. When the glair has set the artist can carry out some preliminary drawing as a guide, using a small soft-hair brush and either a white, or a darkish tone that could be prepared from raw umber with a little white. The brush strokes must be very gentle so as not to disturb the delicate surface of the gold leaf. All the time he must remember that when the actual engraving starts he must exercise a sure and sensitive eye and hand as there is no possibility of making a correction once work has started.

Cennini in his *Il Libro Dell' Arte* written towards the end of the 14th century has a delightful and flowery description of what the unwary artist may be in for. In part this reads:

> There is another way of working on glass ... beautiful, much admired, and exceedingly rare; it is a branch of devotional art in use for the decoration of reliquaries, and calls for sure and ready draughtsmanship.

Cennini then goes on to describe the laying of the gold on the glass with glair and writes:

> When it is quite dry take a very flat wooden tablet covered with black cloth and go into your little workroom where you will not be disturbed. There should be in it but one curtained window.

He then instructs how you should set your table at this window so that the light is over your head when you face towards it. Then after you have laid down the gilded glass on the tablet a very fine pointed needle should be set in a small wooden handle rather like a small brush. The first drawing should be very faint and, having established the composition, the artist should continue working as though using a pen. The darkest tone that can be produced is made by allowing the needle point to go right through the gold leaf. Cennini then comes up with what would seem to be almost an impossibility – he states that half-tones will come when the needle does not quite penetrate the gold. He adds the following comment:

> It must all be done without haste – rather with delight and pleasure. And I give you this advice, that on the day before the day you think of working on this, you hold your hand in a sling or to your bosom, so as to get it all unburdened of blood and rid of fatigue.

When the drawing is completed any intended large areas for showing as black or with colour are scraped away; this can be done today with various blades that will fit in a scalpel handle. Great care has still to be exercised, and it is possible that the painters would have used a small bridge to span the glass and thus keep their hands away from the gold surface and hold them steady when using the needle. The colours could be ground in oil or egg and should be carefully prepared so that they are quite smooth, if the final effect is not to be spoilt. The choice of colours needs care, or the picture may present a garish appearance. Some of the most successful examples have been carried out using only black behind the gold, and great richness can be obtained in this way. A picture worked in the *verre églomisé* technique is very delicate at the back and if it has not already got some form of protection this should certainly be given. The best way to do this is with a piece of hardboard screwed on to the frame so that no part of it touches the back of the glass. It is unwise to start sticking sheets of foil or other substances directly on to the back of the painted and engraved gold because this can easily upset the adhesion of the gold and also will be next to impossible to remove without causing damage.

An interesting example of the forerunners of the technique can be seen with two quite remarkable Roman glass bowls which are in the British Museum. These were found in a tomb at Canosa in Italy and are likely to be Alexandrian work dating from the 1st century BC. The methods used show yet again how advanced the Romans were, especially when handling glass. The gold leaf engraving was protected by a second bowl that was ground to fit exactly over it. Early Christian examples rather interestingly were not always for devotional purposes. The vessels, which were usually rather shallow, have dedications on them to circus heroes as well as saints and one of the commonest inscriptions is 'PIE ZESES' (Drink and live). With these the gold leaf engraving was generally protected by a layer of glass fused below it.

The later Romans inspired a very subtle method with the gold leaf engraving and this was employed to produce some quite remarkable miniature portraits. To obtain very delicate changes in tone values they did not attempt to use line and hatching but employed a fine stippling manner with the needle. A good example of this is in the Museo Cristiano in Brescia where it is set in a Byzantine cross. This is almost certainly genuine, but collectors in this area should beware of the forger who has found many victims with his spurious skills.

In the Victoria and Albert Museum is a quite splendid example that dates from the 14th century. It is Italian although the exact district is open to discussion – Venetian, Sienese, Umbrian and Florentine have been suggested. The subject is the Nativity expressed with the powerful simple sincerity of that period, witness the delightful showing of the washing of the Holy Child in the bottom left-hand corner. This gold engraving is one of a group which appear to all be by the same hand, the most important being a reliquary in the Bargello, Florence. At this time the art of gold engraving outside of Italy seems to have attracted few followers. It was not until the 18th century that more advanced and experimental work was carried out with the technique, although most of the inventive drive was aimed at the decoration of glasses – the so-called *Zwischengoldgläser*. With this approach there was some relationship to the work of the Romans. The vessel forming the inner glass was ground down with considerable precision for about three-quarters of its height, leaving at the top a shoulder projecting. This enabled an outer glass sleeve to be fixed snugly into position and protect the gold decoration on the inner glass.

As a last note on this rigorous but beautiful technique, there was a Dutchman by the name of Zeuner who developed a method using gold and silver foils which covered practically all the glass sheet and gave a mirror-like effect. Into these foils he needled his design, using both stippling and line. The final effect had a quite astonishingly real appearance. Zeuner exhibited with the Society of Artists of Great Britain in 1778; the record gives his address as 28, Haymarket and the item was 'a drawing of a landscape in metals on glass'; it does not give any initial and describes him as a painter of stained glass.

In some ways closely allied to *verre églomisé* but in others a much freer technique is glass painting or what is more literally termed back-glass painting. As with *verre églomisé* it has its origins well back in time. An exact date cannot even be guessed at. Possibly it could have been practised during the 4th or 5th centuries in Byzantium but between this time and when literary evidence in the Middle Ages appears there is little in the way of historical evidence. After this it started to rise in popularity and there were workshops producing examples in at least France, Holland, Spain and Switzerland which were active from the 15th and 16th centuries. Early choice of subjects rested around religious and allegorical themes. Paints used might be either oils or water colours, generally transparent, and they would be laid one on top of another to produce at times lively and attractive effects.

The whole trick with back-glass painting is that the technique of normal painting is reversed – this means that what would be the finishing strokes have to be put on first, for example the highlight in an eye or the sheen on lips, and then the painter works his way towards the distance. With a landscape this means that the sky goes on last after the clouds. Certain sgraffito methods were possible; with these any early layer of colour resting directly on the glass could be scratched and a second colour painted behind; with this treatment the colours would necessarily have to be opaque. Some practioners also liked to paint their figures in first and then lay a covering of mercury behind them so that it gave the feeling the people were in a mirror or in front of one; the method could also be carried out with metal foils. If transparent colours were used some quite strange impressions could be built up.

Back-glass painting had a surge of fashion as a peasant art in the middle of the 19th century with thousands of small primitive pictures being almost mass-produced. The painters kept up a supply of votive paintings for churches and places of pilgrimage; scenes were selected from the New and Old Testaments and saints were portrayed. Travelling salesmen visiting houses sold large quantities of these simple little pictures throughout Europe and also in America; the fashion lasted until the end of the

Top: The oldest paintings known are on the walls of caves and date from around 20,000 BC. This charging bull is from Lascaux in the Dordogne.

Bottom: Detail from a wall painting recently uncovered in the Chapel of the Holy Sepulchre, Winchester Cathedral. It is thought to date from around 1150.

*The Branchini Madonna (c. 1425)
by Giovanni di Paolo.
Egg tempera with
gold ground.*

Top: 'The Adoration of the Magi' (c. 1366) by Luca di Tomme. Egg tempera with gold ground. Bottom: 18th century equestrian portrait of Sir Ralph Gore by James Seymour. Oil on canvas. Shows evidence of several coats of varnish, and a cut, top left, badly repaired.

*The Virgin as Queen of Heaven by Hans Baldung called Gries (c. 1475–1545).
Oil on panel.*

Black and gold engraving on glass, an Italian example of verre églomisé *from the late 14th century.*

Top: 'The isolated rock of Doss Trento' by Albrecht Dürer (1471–1528). Water colour and body colour. Bottom: Cetara, Gulf of Salerno by John Robert Cozens (c. 1752–97). Pencil and water colour.

Top: 'The Field of Waterloo' by Turner (1775–1851). Pen and brown ink and water colour on thin card. Bottom: 'Sunset over the sea' by John Ruskin (1819–1900). Pencil and water colour heightened with white. Both are small scale; the Turner is 8 × 11 in. and the Ruskin 10 × 13 in.

Two water colours painted nearly a hundred years apart. Top: 'Venice: the new Moon' by Turner (1775–1851).

Bottom: 'Venice: Sunset' by Albert Goodwin, 1919.

Top: 'Morpeth Bridge' by Thomas Girtin (1775–1802). Pencil, pen and brown ink and water colour.

Bottom: 'Ightham Mote: the harvesters hurrying away the last of the harvest' by Samuel Palmer (1805–81). Pencil, pen and black ink, water colour and body colour with gum arabic.

Top: Portrait of Rebecca, Lady Rushout (Baroness Northwick) and her three elder children by Daniel Gardner (1750–1805). Pastel and body colour on paper laid on canvas. Bottom: Conversation piece, with the Rev. William Rose, in academic dress, reading to his parents, by Hugh Douglas Hamilton, dated 1775. Black chalk and pastel heightened with white.

Portrait of a girl, probably Elizabeth Seymour, Countess of Ailesbury, by Sir Peter Lely (1618–80). Black, red and white chalk on grey–brown paper.

Portrait of a man wearing a soft broad-brimmed hat (c. 1522) by G. Wolf Huber. Black, red and white chalks.

'Shah Jahan' by Rembrandt (1605–69). Pen and dark brown ink and wash on
Japanese paper washed pale brown.

Esther before Ahasuerus, Burgundian school c. 1430. Pen and brown ink with (partly oxidised) white on pink prepared paper.

Studies of the martyrdom of St George by Paolo Veronese (1528–88). Pen and brown ink and wash.

Ornate frame for a painting now in the Louvre. 'The Music Lesson' by Nicolas Lancret (1690–1743).

19th century and then dropped away as the oleograph came into being.

There was another aspect of back-glass painting and this was the attraction that it had for some sailors and marine artists. These pictures of ships and ports are clearly in another area to the foregoing religious pictures. Marine back-glass paintings started to become popular in the second half of the 18th century – they were a method of expression for those with maritime connections – in some way related to the other crafts of the sea, scrimshaw, ship models, figureheads and carved decoration for the ships. At the start these pictures were an in-thing for those concerned with the oceans; sailors on shore leave ordered them to take home, captains hung them in their homes as a reminder for their families when they were away. The vogue lasted perhaps a few years longer than the votive fashion and when it faded it was for a different reason. In the first few years of this century the sailing ship which made such a fine model for this art form departed from the great oceans. Some of the painters lingered on, bringing their skills to portraying steam ships, but, as these men passed, on so marine back-glass painting ceased. Another chapter in the history of art was locked away in the chest of time.

The techniques of the marine artist in this vein were quite various. The quality of the pictures ranged from poor and crude attempts up to what are truly masterpieces in their field. Many of those at work might never have seen the ships they chose as models so they either had to produce the results from their imagination or to use whatever pictorial aids they could find – engravings, lithographs and latterly photographs, sometimes with the added bonus of accurate descriptions from an eye-witness.

The paints used might be quite crude, possibly enriched shippaint heavy with lead or, with the better examples, oil colours, water colour to which extra gum arabic, size or casein might have been added, various types of tempera and tinted lacquers.

The general method for preparing a picture was first for the artist to work out a detailed drawing of the ship; if he was conscientious, this drawing would be prepared as a mirrored image, so that the ship would be the right way round in the finished picture. He had to put in every little detail, not overlooking matters such as to which sides of the sails the rigging lines ran. Before the actual painting began many would give the back of the glass a thin brushing over with a weak size or diluted varnish. This could act as a form of ground for the paint layers and help them to adhere to the glass.

So the painter could make a start. The first step was to spread the master drawing flat on a board and then place the prepared sheet of glass on top of the drawing. Some method of securing the glass would have to be made as the painting process could take a long time and any movement could endanger the result. The progress of work was as for the other back-glass painting mentioned earlier. Everything had to be in reverse of the usual procedure. Thus the spray and foam lace of the waves could be the first layers, followed by the sea colours that were in front of the ship; including any birds, buoys, floating wreckage. Then the keen eye of the artist must sort out those details on the ship that must be put in before the hull. A sail which may be a comparatively simple matter to paint in the normal manner can become quite complicated when back painted. First must come rigging lines, some of these of course will be behind the sail. At the same time reef points and brails and even all the seams must go in and the shadows that may be on the curved bellies of the sails. So the progress towards the distance goes on, the painter realizing all the time that if a mistake is made the possibility of a satisfactory correction is very small, for it will mean scraping back through the layers of paint and, however carefully this is done, it will probably show at the end.

Some of the painters did use a form of sgraffito with good effect. Small details such as plank lines, rigging, spray and suchlike could be scratched through certain layers and then in-filled with white or the required light tone.

To examine some of these marine masterpieces is to wonder at the skill of the painters – not only with the ships but also particularly with the handling of the skies. Many paintings have subtle graded effects and a thoroughly convincing woolliness of the clouds; all that delicate modelling had to go in *before* the main mass and then be followed by the sky colours. It must have been so easy to overlook a small item like a flying gull or fluttering pennant even when working from a careful drawing. There was one device some of these artists used, and this was to paint the sky, clouds and distant scenes either on to another sheet of glass or paper – working this time the right way round – and then place this behind the back-glass painting. This manner could give a quite deceptive feeling of depth.

Marine glass paintings from the 18th century are today great rarities. The art was not a widespread practice, rather was it centred on a number of places associated with the sea such as the main European ports, with Antwerp as the focal point.

The sad thing with any back-glass painting or *verre églomisé* is that these rather precious and charming works are terribly at risk from careless handling. Often some of the glass sheets they are worked on are too thin for the sheet size and a hard knock or a fall from a rotted picture cord can bring disaster. There is no way that the broken glass can be satisfactorily mended without showing. Some modern adhesives may be able to cement the pieces together but the lovely picture will be forever marred.

Precautions that should be taken include a regular inspection of the hanging cord or wire, and of the fixing devices at the back of the frame. It could help to insert some strips of rubber foam around the edges of the glass where they touch the frame and to put small rubber shock absorbers along the bottom of the frame as they just might absorb enough of the impact in the event of a fall to prevent a breakage.

Lastly, as suggested earlier, have a substantial backing screwed into the frame and, needless to state, if cleaning the front of the glass, be careful to stop any cleaning liquid coming too close to the edge and so seeping round to the back.

Water Colours, Gouache and Mixed Media

To the purist transparent pigments mixed with a gum are water colours; opaque pigments mixed with a gum are gouache colours. But in the history of art the terminology has often become confused, thus water colour can be used to include both transparent and opaque colours when mixed with such diverse substances as gum arabic, gum tragacanth, gall, honey, cherry gum and animal and fish sizes; the one connecting fact being that all the vehicles are water-soluble. The term may also be used collectively for poster colours, showcard colours, distemper colours and powder colours. The principal supports for water colour have always been the various papers available, rag and cartridge, tinted and white and with varying surfaces. The medium has also been used on papyrus by the ancient Egyptians, parchment and vellum by the illuminators, and ivory by miniature painters.

The colours have been largely applied with soft-hair brushes such as sable that were mentioned in an earlier chapter, hog-bristle brushes and sponges have also been used. The appearance of some water colours often leads people to think that the medium is simple to work with. This is quite erroneous; in fact water colour is a difficult method. This is primarily because the colours are mostly transparent and have to be applied *alla prima*, and do not take kindly to attempts at retouching or correction. Most painters work placing dark colours into light and bear in mind that the lightest tone in a painting is the colour of the paper – when dry the light penetrates the translucent paints and is reflected from the paper underneath. To achieve the full effect of this many artists prefer to work on a white paper. Unless working on very heavy rag papers or what are termed 'pasteless boards', the paper is always stretched on a board; this is done by wetting both sides, easing it down flat, and sticking the edges with paper tape. As the paper dries out it will become drum tight and will be unlikely to buckle when heavy washes are applied.

In many ways water colour can be more various than any of the other media; it can achieve great subtleties with the rendering of atmosphere, light, reflected light, soft mists, passing showers, turbulent storms. It can present the greatest delicacy of nuance or, with someone like Turner or Nolde, the full punching power of an unleashed palette. There is no historical connection between the water-colour painting on vellum of the medieval illuminators and the modern practice.

The techniques recognised today developed largely from the drawings which the painters from the 15th to the 17th century were constantly making in the most varied media. Among these methods was the strengthening of an outline drawing with a pen with a slight wash of colour which was often a warm brown. Another formative manner was the progress of the brush and wash technique, which can itself be traced to the influence of the Far Eastern ink paintings. Water colour has always held pride of place with the artists of China and Japan and it is with this elusive technique that their greatest painting triumphs have been won.

If any one person can claim to be the founder of modern water-colour painting this must surely be Albrecht Dürer (1471–1528), the master of print-making and of the handling of oil, tempera, silver-point, pen and ink, charcoal, crayon and water colour. With his small study of 'The isolated rock of Doss Trento with the Romanesque Church of St Appollinare di Piedicastello' (it measures $6\frac{5}{8} \times 8\frac{3}{8}$ in), he presages manners of later masters of the medium with his understanding of transparent water colour allied to bodycolour. Nearly a century on Sir Peter Paul Rubens (1577–1640) employed similar methods for studies of his large oil landscapes. But the examples of such work are sparse in the lead up to the 18th century when the British School of Water Colourists came into being. One after another protagonist in this demanding technique came into the limelight.

The early painters worked out the problems with monochrome, then progressed by applying neutral tints, a transparent wash of cool grey being used for the sky and distance and a comparatively warm brown tint for the foreground. This gentle treatment was to a degree pioneered by John Robert Cozens (1752–1797) exemplified by pictures that he painted on a trip to Italy, particularly those of Swiss scenes. Sadly in 1794 he became mentally ill but he and his family were generously supported by the Royal Academy, Sir George Beaumont and Dr Monro.

Contemporary with him and following on came a team of

painters who were to give a supremacy to the British School that was to last well into the 19th century. The leaders were Paul Sandby (1725–1809), John Crome (1768–1821), John Sell Cotman (1782–1842), Thomas Girtin (1775–1802), David Cox (1775–1851) and the incomparable Joseph Mallord William Turner (1775–1851).

As diverse as the manners are with oil painting, an examination of water colours from this period shows in many ways even wider experimentation. Each individual has an approach which can be recognised with practice; the 'handwriting' of the brush can stand out more clearly than with oils and even in the handling of washes for skies and other broad areas there are innumerable nuances that can be discerned. Painters became entranced by the possibilities of the transparent colours and the almost infinite variations of tint and tone that opened up for them. It was found that the different papers offered chances for experimenting – dry they could impart a crispness, lightly dampened a softening, quite moist a chance for 'bleeding' and grading the colours one in to the other.

W. H. Pyne, a contemporary worker with water colour and a writer on art had some enlightening points over Girtin of whom he wrote that he:

> prepared his drawings on the same principle which had hitherto been confined to painting in oil, namely, laying in the object upon his paper with the local colour, and shading the same with the individual tint of its own shadow. Previous to the practice of Turner and Girtin, drawings were shaded first entirely through, whatever their component parts – houses, cattle, trees, mountains, foregrounds, middle-ground and distances, all with black or grey, and these objects were afterwards stained or tinted, enriched or finished, as is now the custom to colour prints. It was the new practice, introduced by these distinguished artists, that acquired for designs in water-colours upon paper the title of paintings.

As with oil painters of the later 18th century and the first half of the 19th century, water-colour painters sometimes reached out too far when they investigated strange substances that might be used for pigments. The most macabre of these must be 'mummy', which might consist chiefly of bone ash, asphaltum and the textile wrappings and other materials used in the preparation of the mummy. These substances were ground up – the resulting colour being a rather pleasant warm brown somewhat like a light-toned burnt umber. Mixed with a gum and water it could give a fair wash but was very unreliable and almost certain to fade. Despite horror mongers it is improbable that the mummified flesh was ground down, it is much more likely that the asphaltum was chipped off the bindings. Apparently artists in many cases were in ignorance as to how their colour makers produced this delightful shade. When they found out the colour went out of fashion rather speedily. Today and for some years the pilfering of tombs for the benefit of the painter has been illegal, although odd limbs may sometimes be found in the laboratories of the manufacturers. A publication brought out in 1886 gives the following details:

Mummy or Egyptian Brown
Chemical Names and Composition White pitch and myrrh combined with animal matter.
Artistic Qualities A rich transparent colour.
Conditions of Permanency It is less liable to crack and move on the canvas than asphaltum.
Conditions of Non-Permanency It is a substance better rejected from the palette, as no reliance can be placed on it.
General Adulterations Its organic origin renders it liable to contain ammonia and particles of fat in a concrete state, which are undesirable.
Remarks Bodies were embalmed 3,000 years ago in liquid bitumen. It is this bitumen, combined with parts of the body, that compose mummy brown.

Less exotic but just as dangerous for the palette was sap green. It was prepared from the inspissated (which rather weird-sounding word means only thickened and condensed) juice of buckthorn berries, or the leaves of woad or the blue flowers of the iris. It gave a rich yellowish-green that was prone to fade, but if found on a colour maker's list today it will have been prepared synthetically. The search for rich bright colours led many into risky practices. There was *iodine scarlet*, an iodide of mercury that impressed some with its good body and opacity; a magnificent scarlet, one writer says, unequalled by any other pigment. But this colour was easily decomposed by other pigments, foul air destroyed the scarlet tint and light caused it to fade. Another warm brown that attracted some followers was bistre. This was prepared from charred beechwood, but the resulting pigment could contain impurities and coarse particles of soot and ash; it could encourage mildew and was liable also to fade and to attract moisture from the atmosphere. The search for a strong, warm, dark brown went on, probably because burnt umber and burnt sienna, rich and powerful as they were, did not have the quality of partial or complete transparency that was needed. The colour makers started using large quantities of extract from cuttlefish, the ink-sacs of which provided a semi-transparent, very dark rich brown. Sepia, as this tint was known, was quite unsuitable for oils, but did find a place on the palette for water colour. Although not totally permanent to light, sepia is a very pleasant colour to work with, particularly with washes as varying dilutions with water will bring up attractive tints.

Bearing in mind such adventures with their materials it is not surprising that a number of water-colour as well as oil paintings, which have been discussed in chapter four, look a little strange. Fading can do several things, apart from loss of strength it can also, to a degree, change the character of a colour and so alter the whole relationship of colour harmonies intended by the painter. In an endeavour to halt the ravages of light, some artists tried protective measures which sometimes did little more than darken the tints they were supposed to protect and at the worst could wreck a picture. A gentleman called Nicholson in a publication 'Practice' recommended applying a varnish that would lock up the pigments, presumably he thought securely. All that actually happened was that there was an overall darkening so that the water colour lost much of its prime quality of luminosity, there was also a chance that the frail paint layer could dis-integrate – further, the varnish would be next to impossible to remove.

Any works in water colour or mixed media containing water colour should be treated with care. On no account should direct sunlight be allowed to fall upon them, in fact where possible they should be hung on a wall facing north; over-bright artificial light should be avoided and, if they are ultra-delicate, it is wisest to have a small blind over the frame or even to keep them in a port-folio. If that unpleasant malady, 'foxing', appears – it shows initially as small orange-brown spots – do not be tempted to follow some of the recipes that are around for bleaching out this menace. Leave the treatment to a conservator as it is easy to cause damage to pictures which may be in a fragile condition. Likewise if there are tears or other physical damages, seek a trained hand.

Such marring of the surface of some water colours could have arisen from instructions given in early painting manuals. One brought out in 1839 advocates some hazardous procedures. It suggests rubbing a wet cloth over the surface of some colours to give a granulated appearance, and stroking with a wet brush any areas that appear too sharp. Further it says that areas of dark tones may be cleared by laying on water and pressing in bread crumbs. But any muddling about with the surface of a pure water colour during painting or afterwards will almost inevitably destroy that beautiful sparkling freshness which is the true attraction for the collector. For an *aquarelle* – the term used by the purist water-colour painter – achieves its effect by the glazing qualities of the colours used, and those colours rest on the paper in the very thinnest of layers. Any tinkering with these minute veils afterwards is bound to mar them.

For many painters working on an *aquarelle*, preparatory measures such as drawing in, even with the faintest of pencil lines, would be rejected. In a way an *aquarelle* has a relationship to a fresco, for on a much smaller scale it demands that same directness and abandoned courage – the painter must have the picture clear in his mind and then go straight in with the brush. This approach to the medium is not one that can be lingered over, it asks for decision and speed; two characteristics that, once achieved, enable the artist to capture light, fleeting colour and the movement of nature.

Cotman could instil into a landscape an almost breathless purity as he laid on his washes – a thin skim of exactly the right tint of colour for water could suggest great depth of the swiftly-moving scurries of fresh spring runs over the shallows. By his overlaying of tones in woodlands each successive brush sweep gave a feeling of reaching into the dark foliage, of the chance to feel one's way deeper and deeper into the forest. His clouds have that wraith-like wispy substance that they should have as on a hot day they float over a peerless clear blue sky which grades down to a soft misty pink at the skyline.

Crome, who was also a powerful oil painter, relied on the water-colour sketch to find the foundation for many of his larger canvases. 'Old Crome', as this interesting man became known, was born in Norwich, the son of a journeyman weaver. He lived his early years in poor circumstances, probably having little in the way of education. It is recorded that when twelve years old he set out on life by being the errand boy for a Dr Rigby, the local physician in Norwich. A short spell of this and he tired of carting round medicine bottles and apprenticed himself for seven years to a Frank Whistler who was a house and sign painter in the city, and was to continue for a while with the same man as a journeyman. Thence he doggedly set out to follow some innate sense that pointed him towards painting. He was to be brought into contact with Sir William Beechey, a collector and patron of the arts, who allowed the young fellow access to his collection. Crome took every advantage of this and thus gained a very large part of his art instruction from studying the Dutch and Flemish masters – for his subsistence he took a job teaching wherever he found the opportunity. To him must be given much of the credit for the founding of the East Anglian School; in 1803 he, with several amateurs and young artists, brought into being 'The Norwich Society of Artists' for the purpose of encouraging a love of the Fine Arts and forwarding artistic culture. An examination of his water-colour sketches shows the alert observation he possessed, for he rarely missed any detail of foliage, streams, old buildings or skies. He travelled but little in England and Wales; he made only one trip across the Channel to Belgium and France and appears to have got no further south than Paris. Most of all he was content to record the particular colours and textures of that flat landscape of East Anglia and to live in the company of his friends. Deeply influenced by the Dutch landscape painters, as he passed onward the painter in him is said to have murmured: 'Hobbema, my dear Hobbema, how I have loved you!'

It is the variety of manners which so draws many to acquiring water colours, each statement can be a contrast which stimulates the imagination and weds the appreciation of the owner to the inspiration of the artist – what more joyous consummation visually can there be for a room? As diverse as painters are in themselves, possibly subconsciously, this state is encouraged by the individuality of taste of the collector. In the appreciation of art, surely there must be somewhere something for everyone. How the pulse can quicken as a gallery is visited and the eye lights on a certain work that mutely beckons to some deep lying trait! The cool measured strokes of John Robert Cozens or his like may appeal but not excite, the accomplishments of Girtin may be admired or it may be that the search is for the work of David Cox. A contrast with many of his contemporaries, Cox had that particular magic when working at his best which could work wonders with a landscape. The winds really blow through his trees, the fingers of an evening breeze ruffle through the grass; it seems that he could give life to every part of a scene. In

1805 he made his first visit to Wales, going to many of the romantic parts of the Principality, and ever afterwards the Welsh scene with its ragged looming mountains, turbulent waters and evening-purpled beacons was his favourite above all other locations. In 1813 he was elected to the Society of Painters in Water Colours and in the year following he started to teach at the Military College at Farnham. But he was not happy pinned down so far from those delights of Wales, and he took a post at a ladies' school in Hereford just across the border from the Welsh scene. He left behind him some hundred oil paintings and a very large number of water colours – the exact number would be very difficult to work out, largely because he was one who, like the French Corot, drew the attentions of many copyists and outright fakers. But it if were possible to hang a supposed Cox beside a true Cox, surely in a very brief time that excited feeling that David Cox could generate in a picture would overwhelm the false one. This plagiarism of style is by no way a rarity, it is an unpleasant blurring fog that follows talent; sometimes slyly and sometimes blatantly, feeding off a reflected glory. It can only be defeated by knowledge, by studying the work of the chosen and comparing the whole manner of working. In many ways a water colour is one of the hardest subjects for a forger to ape. Spontaneity is the heart of water-colour painting, and this may well be the quality that will defeat the crook who must labour to simulate the strokes often emotively applied by the real painter.

In contrast to the restless energy of David Cox, an instructive comparison can be made with Thomas Girtin, another painter who has drawn his share of copyists. His approach in general has already been mentioned, but it is his mature style (if that can be the name for the later work of one who was so sadly removed whilst still in his twenty-seventh year) that thrills the connoisseur. Thomas when a boy had a close friendship with Turner and they are recorded as sketching together scenes beside the Thames and copying old masters in the collection of Dr Monro. As his prowess surged forward he drew his influence less from English painters such as Sandby, Hearne and Dayes than from an earlier period. Girtin's influence goes back to the powerhouse manner with landscapes of Rubens, wedding these impressions to the powerful perspective compositions of Canaletto, and softening both these two with the genuine deep romanticism of Richard Wilson who was born some sixty years before him. In the time that was granted to him, Girtin made strides towards that perfection which he must have glimpsed. His travels took him over much of England and Wales; favourite subjects included ruined castles and abbeys and the moorlands and mountains of Yorkshire, Northumberland and the Welsh landscape. At the end he journeyed to Paris to find a strength for his weakening health, but he was too late. Few artists can be considered to have progressed farther in such a short span as Girtin, and it must have been this consideration that caused Turner to exclaim, 'If Tom Girtin had lived, I should have starved'.

The painters mentioned in detail have each given some part of the integral whole of water colour; there is one artist who alone presents an almost total appreciation of all that this medium can give the painter and the viewer. Born in the same year as Girtin, Joseph Mallord William Turner was to share the brilliant promise of his friend and to take it farther than anything that had been done with landscape before. To study in a gallery a comprehensive collection of his work is to have a chance to understand almost all the ways of water colour, from the smallest of sketches to the large studies which challenge the senses with the sheer power of their conception and execution. Girtin, as Turner himself acknowledged, had the touch of genius; a quality that was the key for Turner. The muse within the boy was active before he went to school, and the earliest recorded work is a picture of Margate church drawn when he was nine. Not long after this he was exhibiting copies of engravings that he had made, taking advantage of his father's barbershop window. In quick succession in his teens he spent a spell colouring prints for John Raphael Smith, in making drawings at Dr Monro's, in washing-in backgrounds for a Mr Porden, and in the studio of Thomas Malton junior, an architect, who dismissed him for an inability to learn perspective – an interesting happening bearing in mind that some years later he was to be Professor of Perspective at the Royal Academy.

Mr Cosmo Monkhouse comments on the education of Turner:

> He learnt reading from his father, writing and probably little else at his schools at Brentford and Margate, perspective (Imperfectly) from T. Malton, architecture (imperfectly and classical only) from Mr Hardwick, water-colour drawing from Dr Monro and perhaps some hints as to painting in oils from Sir Joshua Reynolds, in whose house he studied for a while.

At fourteen he was admitted as a student at the Royal Academy School and in the same year he showed a 'View of the Archbishop's Palace at Lambeth'.

At the youthful age of twenty-four he was elected an Associate of the Royal Academy, reaching full membership in 1802. The bright sun of his glory had begun to rise. Between then and 1851 Turner worked at his art as few have before him or since. His total output runs into thousands. He travelled constantly over Britain and much of Europe carrying the impedimenta of his trade; the logistics of obtaining his art materials and that of transporting his easels, boards, water-bottles, brushes, paints, papers, a stool, rags etc. must have been a major problem.

The work of this man can very broadly be divided into three stages. Within him quite possibly glowed one of the strongest lights of pure unassailable genius granted to any painter. So he drove himself forward through early conquests of a natural realism in the tradition of Gainsborough; later travelling through France he discovered Poussin and explored the realms of mythology as a subject for imaginative expression; then he came, suddenly it seems, out into the vastness of light and atmosphere. During the middle period John Ruskin made a somewhat strange comment on Turner's manner, he said:

> it is now stern, reserved, quiet, grave in colour, forceful in hand. His mind tranquil; fixed, in physical study, on the Mythology of Homer, and the Law of the Old Testament.

As the years went past Turner gave himself solely to challenging nature. There were times when he must have waited for just that instant of elemental fact to be exposed before him – the force of a rising storm, the biting cold of wind-hurled snowflakes, the lurid glare of wild flames. Above all he showed those magic moments when a rainstorm passes and the hot sun pours through to simmer the soaked turf, sending up a silver haze through which the landscape looses substance to become something else. Turner not only could see these things; but by his seeing has given it to us in his paintings.

Look closely at some of his later and more exciting large water colours and glimpse the battlefield from which this man wrested his achievement. The paper may bear scars from abrasion, even small slashes with a sharp point, overpaints, overglazes, scumbling, opaque body colours and brush strokes that today still carry the vigour and attack of this man. Further and further he pushed this pursuit of the elements, until the sheer force of what he could paint almost evokes the total sound and fury, or on the other hand, the amazing gentle peace of a late afternoon when the evening light begins to stream in raking silver beams across some stretch of water. Perhaps there may be one lonely boat on that water: it will appear suspended, anchored in a mystic haze that shimmers across the background and melts the rooftops and church spire of the distant village into a violet blur.

His last few years found him leaving his house in Queen Anne Street and his faithful housekeeper Mrs Danby to live in a small house in Chelsea with one called Sophia Caroline Booth; he adopted the name Booth for himself. In 1851 his executor, following leads from Mrs Danby, found Turner there on 18 December and on the next day Turner died. It seemed that he had said almost all that could be said with water colour.

Many painters owe much to Turner who gave them the courage to disregard academic rulings as to what could and what could not be done when working with water colour – it was the final picture that their work would be judged by. The medium broadened out as more and more body colour was used, at first this was a heavy opaque Chinese white. To start with it was somewhat timorously used, almost just as heightening, and then it became an integral part of the picture and gouache colours came to the artist's palette. Some started to add hog-bristle brushes to their quiver and mild forms of impasto came to be used. This had to be kept in check because if too thick the gouache colours would crack and lose their adhesion to the paper. Tinted papers became popular and with gouache the underlying tints of these papers could be employed in the same manner as the *imprimatura* with oil painting. Exciting effects were possible with the lighter tones of some colours against these coloured supports. More and more painters emulated Turner's unrestricted manipulation of the paints across the surface of the paper – erasers could be used to rub in rays of light, sandpaper would produce broken textures, and experiment could be made into the interesting effects of 'wax resist' – with this a piece of wax would be rubbed over parts of the picture which, when a wash of colour was applied, resulted in speckled textures.

Adventures into 'mixed media' were made where two or more methods of colour application were involved in obtaining the result the artist wanted. At the beginning these experiments were little more than the pen-and-ink wash drawings of some of the earlier masters. As the idea progressed examples can be found that show water colour with pastel work on top, or sometimes the other way round with the water colour over the pastel. Others worked pastel into heavy gouache and possibly even pen and ink as well; egg tempera they found went well with water colour; it was also used sometimes in rather risky ways for the permanence of the painting with oils. Some intrepid souls even tried to make pastels stay on the surface of oils. Heavily diluted oils were used with pen and ink, and, strangest of all, *frottage*, the technique of taking a rubbing on paper of an underlying object, was developed by the early Surrealists. Max Ernst (1891–1976) was one who explored the idea of combining the rubbed image and other graphic methods with painting. He was seeking to find some visual stimulus for his subconscious. In his 'The Origin of the Pendulum' it shows that he rubbed rough boards for parts of the design.

A painting which gives the appearance of being worked in two or more media should be examined carefully. At times some artists can get carried away with the excitement of colour effects and texture build-ups and use substances that are just not going to be at all lasting. If there are undue signs of cracking in a recently completed picture, or flaking or other signs of deterioration, it may be best to take advice from a conservator because some 'mixed media' works can be extremely difficult to treat. In this category really has to come collage because it can contain various aspects of water-colour painting. The word collage was derived from the French, meaning to paste or stick down, and the manner evolved from *papiers collés*, a 19th-century leisure pastime. Kurt Schwitters, a Surrealist, did considerable work in this manner early in this century. The trouble with collages is that they can combine so many different materials that they are a nightmare for the conservator – often consisting of water colour, paper pieces stuck on and textiles, gouache, acrylics, household paint, wood shavings, metal pieces, waxes, varnishes – the ultimate in mixed media.

There were two highly individual figures who between them span from about the middle of the 18th century to the latter part of the 19th. These were Blake and Palmer. William Blake (1757–1827), who has been mentioned in an earlier chapter as the gadfly for poor Sir Joshua Reynolds, was born in London, the second son of a hosier of Broad Street, Golden Square. At the age of ten he was studying at Pars' Drawing Academy in the Strand; this was followed by an apprenticeship as an engraver and later he worked with James Basire as a draughtsman. A strange individualistic character, Blake moved out into a secret world of his own, one peopled by visions and fantasies. He painted largely with forms of water colour, sometimes alone and sometimes mixed with tempera. The particular effects he achieved bear signs of a technique not worked by anyone else. He also developed an off-beat method which he termed his 'fresco', this consisted basically of working from a ground of glue and whiting on canvas. Ruskin came up with one of his statements that are a little difficult to understand when he said of the painter: 'In expressing conditions of glaring and flickering light, Blake is greater than Rembrandt.' This man who gave much – not only with his depiction of scenes that were a revelation but also coupled with them some great poetic lines – on the twelfth of August of his last year went on his way 'singing of the things he saw in heaven'.

Samuel Palmer (1805–1881) was of a different mould. The world that he showed in his water colours and oils had an atmosphere of its own, often the time chosen being late in the day or even at night. He liked to paint with a free method of gouache, generally overlaid on preparatory work in water colour, and in some of his pictures there is evidence of the workings of his mind as the painting progressed. Swirls of pencil lines, jabs of thick paint to obliterate early details – but with that seeming magic of some of the 'way-out' masters the whole comes together in the end. A Palmer can be a stimulating experience when examined closely because, in its own way, it can be a lesson in technique. His output of paintings and drawings was quite considerable and this work was supplemented by a number of etchings, including illustrations for Virgil's *Eclogues*.

In the 20th century there has been one man who can claim to challenge the supposition that Turner had said it all with water colour. This is the German Emil Nolde, a founder of the Expressionist movement in his country. Although he was born in 1867 and lived until 1956, it is the work that he did in this century which was so explosively revolutionary. If Turner had witnessed what Nolde did with water colour he must surely have rubbed his hands together with sheer joy at the daring of the man. Nolde founded the *Neue Sezession* in Berlin and was associated with *Die Brücke* and the *Blaue Reiter*, but despite these associations there was no one else who worked in his manner. He drew on folk tales and religious motifs for his influence and inspiration. At the start his colour was muted, his forms were broad and the drawing was with a large and free brush. As his confidence grew, so the colour warmed, gathered strength and rose upward in a glorious movement of vibrant tones and tints that had a power that earlier painters would not have thought possible with water colour. He painted also in oils, but it is the amazing richness of his full-blooded water colours and gouaches that are so appealing and utterly satisfying. Pungent floods of indigo sweep across the paper colliding with brushstrokes of liquid cadmium orange, luscious wet greens are laid alongside full-strenth cadmium reds. When he was ordered to stop painting by the Nazis, in secret he worked on producing his *'Ungemalte Bilder'*, hundreds of small water-colour studies – some of which he worked up into full-size paintings after the war. With his bold manner with water colour, Emil Nolde perhaps broke through a final barrier towards his freedom and has given great joy in colour to many.

The Techniques
for Drawing

The diversity of the tools and the ways that an artist can handle them make drawings for many collectors one of the most fascinating areas of pictorial expression. The smallest 'thumb nail' sketch roughed in with a few pencil lines can be the most intimate sign to a painter's intention, giving form to an idea as the hand reaches out.

The clarity of line is something which can be evident whether from the steel nib of a pen, the stroke of a crayon, or even when masked to a degree by a brush and wash, or in a finished pastel drawing. There is a naked purity about many drawings which can make their acquisition almost irresistible; the artist is at times baring his soul. Probably in the majority of cases he may never even have thought the drawings would leave his studio. They were done for his private purpose, as experiments with compositional arrangements, posing of figures, working out ideas that would later be incorporated in a full-size finished painting. Many painters have preferred to make small drawings when working on a landscape and then, in the refuge of their studio, have constructed the intended picture from these.

Drawings very often have a quality that is difficult to define; it can be something that is subtle but at the same time brims with the sparkle of life and vitality – perhaps with some sketches it is because the artist tends to dash them off freely and is not worried by the problems of the commissioned picture. To examine and understand the techniques that have been used can increase the appreciation of these works, for drawings can express so much, often by economic means, that cannot be clarified by words.

Pastel
A method of drawing (sometimes referred to as painting) with sticks of dry colour which have the minimum of binder – one reason why pastel pictures keep their bright fresh look almost

indefinitely. A number of the earlier ones may not have been fixed, thus they should be handled carefully as a slight knock may cause particles of colour to fall off the paper. The pastel sticks are composed of pure pigment mixed with an inert filler such as kaolin with a minimal amount of gum tragacanth, casein or skimmed milk, and they are formed into sticks by extrusion or a pressure mould. Today each colour can be bought in different depths of tone. The technique for most is to use the desired tint and tone straight on to the paper and not to mix two colours together on the paper.

Pastel is essentially a direct medium. Any preliminary drawing with a pencil should be kept to the minimum, many use faint charcoal lines as these will soon be lost in the progressing picture. As far as possible pastel should not be touched once it has been laid on the paper; but some choose to manipulate the colours with soft-hair and hog-bristle brushes, finger tips and paper stumps; small pieces of chamois and soft erasers have also been employed. There are a number of papers, white and tinted, that have been used and these include: Canson, Ingres, Montgolfier, soft rag papers like Cox, De Wint and Turner. The main point is that the paper should have a certain grain to it that will drag the pigment particles off the pastel as it is applied and hold them in place. The pastels should be soft and crumble easily between finger and thumb; if they are hard and brittle they will not work well and will produce an unpleasant scratched surface. The artist specialising in pastel will probably have a box with upwards of two hundred sticks in it.

One of the most difficult problems with pastel is with regard to fixing; if this is not done, as mentioned above the pictures will remain fragile. It is claimed by a number of artists that applying a fixative will tend to bring down the values of the tints and also may considerably alter the tones, blues and browns darkening. Modern synthetic fixatives should be safe but if in doubt with a valuable pastel drawing consult an expert.

A pastel should have a thick mount so that the drawing can be kept well away from the glass. Hang them so that direct light from the sun does not fall across the picture and also in a position not exposed to heat from fires or radiators. Be careful that the wall is dry and there is no danger of rising damp. Certainly inspect the drawings regularly for signs of 'foxing' or mould growths or other signs of deterioration. Treatment for a stained pastel or other damage is strictly the province of the conservator and never attempt it yourself as serious damage can be caused very quickly. Modern methods in the restoration studio do allow for the cleaning and bleaching of pastels.

The origin of the medium lies with the heightening and tinting of pen-and-ink and charcoal drawings by such artists as Leonardo da Vinci, Dürer and Holbein the Younger, they used white and red chalks for the purpose. But pastel as an independent medium did not evolve until the 18th century. The position is complicated by the fact that in the early periods a pastel was called a crayon. Credit for the development is claimed for at least three people: Mme Vernerin and Mlle Heid (1688–1753) both of Danzig, also Johann Alexander Thiele (1685–1752), a landscape painter and skilled etcher; Rosalba Carriera of Venice (1675–1757) was another who was much concerned with the perfecting of the manner, there were 157 drawings in pastel by her in the Dresden Museum.

From early in the 18th century Paris was a fashionable centre for practising pastel; artists of the quality of Boucher, Watteau, Greuze, Nattier, Drouais and Quentin de Latour (1704–1788). This last artist was considered to be one of the finest exponents of the medium, particularly with portraits, and at one time had had no less than eighty-five examples in the museum at St Quentin. Pastels as a medium for landscape were used by Simon Mathurin Lantara (1729–1778), he liked to present sunsets, moonlight nights and seascapes; Joseph Vernet sometimes added the figures to the compositions. Another portrait artist in the medium was Jean Baptiste Perroneau (1731–1796) whose 'Jeune Fille au Chat' is a favourite for many when visiting the Louvre.

The use of pastel in England started earlier than in France and the likes of John Riley (1646–1691) were active with portraits. In the following century one of the finest hands with this fragile medium was Francis Cotes (c. 1725–1770) who had worked under the tutelage of Rosalba Carriera; his flesh tones were somewhat cool and chalky but the likenesses he achieved were apparently successful. Cotes was thought to be eclipsed in excellence by one of his pupils John Russell (1745–1806) who had bought from Carriera her four fine pictures entitled 'The Seasons' and on these he fashioned his style. Russell was diverse in his subjects for, apart from portraits, he produced 'conversation pieces', historical scenes and what were termed 'fancy' pictures. In Ireland there was Hugh Hamilton who made a good trade with small under life-size oval portraits mostly worked in grey, red and black. Up to this time many of the most successful pastel artists had practised the habit of smoothing and blending their colours together with almost imperceptible gradations. The Englishman Ozias Humphry (1742–1810) broke with this habit and made a point of letting his individual pastel strokes be seen. The miniaturist Richard Cosway experimented with the medium and produced at least one good portrait, this was of George, Prince of Wales; his wife Maria had more success as her touch had more delicacy. In the 19th century there was a decline of the medium and about the only user of quality was Henry Bright (1814–1873) whose landscapes received much praise. In France, certainly in the latter part of the 19th century and into the 20th, the technique was given a lift by Hilaire Germain Edgar Degas (1834–1917) who used the medium in particular to catch superbly much of the atmosphere of the ballet. Henri Raymonde de Toulouse-Lautrec (1864–1901) was another who used the bright fragile colours to great effect with many of his drawings of the night life of Paris. Both of the foregoing artists at times employed pastels as part of a mixed media either with water colour or forms of gouache. The art of pastel, as M. Roger Ballu put it, 'was slumbering a little', but then in 1870 the Société des Pastellistes was founded in France and met with a welcome. Apart from Degas and Lautrec others found the attractions of the medium: Millet, Lhermitte, Moreau, Besnard, Machard, Picard, and Brochard, who was successful at applying pastels to vellum; in Belgium there was Émile Wauters who was noted for life-size portraits of both men and women that were quite amazing with their strength and richness of colour. In Italy the practice was taken up by artists such as Laurenti, Fragiacomo and Segantini; in Holland Josselin de Jong; in Germany Von Lenbach and Max Liebermann and in Norway Fritz Thaulow.

The revival fashion crossed the Channel and in 1880 the Pastel Society held its first exhibition in the Grosvenor Gallery; but this turned out to be a false start and the society nearly faded until it was reconstituted in 1899. Then regular contributors to the exhibitions included: E. A. Abbey, J. M. Swan, J. J. Shannon, Sir James Guthrie, H. Brabazon, Walter Crane, Edward Stott, S. J. Solomon and W. Rothenstein.

Chalk and Crayon
Principally three colours have been used, white, red and black. The material became popular with artists during the Renaissance period when the white and red were used to give a 'heightening' effect to pen-and-ink drawings and also to black

chalk work. Although these chalks were soft and would smudge quite easily, they were preferred by many to charcoal as the pigment particles would adhere better to the papers used. Some users prepared their papers by giving them a coat of weak starch or size and then, when this was still tacky, they sprinkled a light dusting of a substance such as pumice powder over the surface. Once this was hardened it made possible not only strong clean strokes with the chalks but also ensured that the chalks would have a better hold on the paper.

The early chalks would have been without any binder but later small quantities of substances such as those employed when making pastels were added and the range of colours was increased. Confusion arises once more because there is talk of red crayon work which in the earlier times would have been termed red chalk. In the 18th century Antoine Watteau (1684–1721) had a great skill with his handling of the red crayon or *sanguine* as it was becoming known; his portrait and costume sketches had a beautiful delicacy about them, an effect achieved very often with much economy of line.

The French mechanical genius, chemist and painter Nicolas Jaques Conté (1755–1805) introduced sticks of compressed chalk and pigment with a binder. These were grease free and can still be obtained today, colours include: sanguine, black, bistre and white. Conté researched into drawing materials for the artist, as owing to the war with England France was deprived of much of her supplies of plumbago; Conté substituted for it a mixture of graphite and clay and took out a patent for the product in 1795 and the pencil still bears his name.

The Conté chalks or crayons, as they are more commonly called today, come in small sticks about three inches long which are square in section. This square end lends itself to numerous variations of line when applied; the crayons are delightful to work with on a great variety of papers and will to a degree hold on well without fixing. But if fixing is done, great care needs to be taken that the fixing liquid does not flood the crayons off the paper.

Crayons for artists to work with today come in a rather bewildering array: round, square and hexagonal in section, some are even triangular. They may be dry bound with some water soluble substance or quite heavily bound with waxes. The range of colours available can run up to nearly a hundred tints. Some have no covering, others may be paper wrapped or in wood casings. There are also water-colour crayons that may be wood cased or left unwrapped; these will be water soluble and can give interesting effects when worked into dampened paper with a water-colour painting. A few years ago there came so-called oil chalks or pastels; these are messy to use although the colours available are rich and strong. But the resulting work will easily smudge and the drawings are practically impossible to fix – thus the oil pastel is really most suitable for school use.

Charcoal

One of the oldest drawing materials, in truth it really spans time from the caveman right through till today. There is written evidence that the early Greeks used the method and there are scribbles in charcoal on the walls of some of the houses at Pompeii.

Charcoal is the blackish residue consisting of impure carbon obtained by removing the volatile constituents of animal and vegetable substances. Artist's charcoal is made from woods of varying types, and the method of preparation dates back to a remote period. Logs are piled into a conical heap, with a central shaft to act as a flue and openings at the bottom to admit air. The whole is then covered with sodden turf and soil. The firing starts at the bottom and gradually spreads through the logs, and the operation depends on a controlled rate of combustion and the temperatures reached. Wood becomes brown at 220°C and a deep brown-black at 280°C. The different woods give varying characteristics to the resulting charcoal. Willow is one of the commonest for the artist's use but it does need to be sifted through as some of the twigs can be brittle and over hard, peach wood and lime wood have also been tried, but the best of all, if it is well prepared, is vine charcoal. This can give a beautiful velvet rich black.

A drawing carried out with charcoal can achieve extraordinary sensitivity of tone and at the same time a powerful chiaroscuro with deep blacks. The surface has an attractive, dry, very slight sheen, the half-tones display delicate silvery greys not achieved by other media. The charcoal is best broken up into small pieces and, if desired, it can be wrapped in scraps of paper to keep the fingers clean or it may be held in what is called a 'porte crayon' made from metal or slips of bamboo. Once on the paper the charcoal can be manipulated in the same way as pastel and chalk with paper stumps, hog brushes or a fragment of chamois. Erasers such as plastic rubbers or art gum may be used to lighten areas and induce the effect of light rays, reflected lights or highlights. The most suitable papers include those mentioned for pastel; tinted ones usually give the best results – light brown, dull yellow or soft grey. The drawing will need some form of fixing, particularly if it is in vine charcoal as it will smudge easily. Fixing, however, will not affect the tonal values.

Although many artists will just use charcoal for rough sketches and preparing large layouts for murals, it has been used with great success for portraits and figure studies. Albrecht Dürer realised the possibilities of the subtle qualities that could be released by careful shading; in 1514 he did a study of his mother which exemplifies the best of charcoal and shows how the effect it achieves lies between the cool steely appearance of pencil and the richer Conté crayon. The medium does lend itself to heightening with white chalk and, at times, additional work with red or brown chalks. It has been used successfully as an under-drawing for water-colour wash and will give pleasant bleeding tones to the water colour; also the washes will tend to fix the charcoal.

Oriental Ink Drawing

For some collectors this has a special place, partly because its origins are apart from those drawing techniques that have been developed in the West. Painting and drawing pictorially in the Far East are primarily the product of calligraphy and this influence can be traced through the compositions of most draw-ings and paintings. Some of the most delightful pictures are those that combine a drawing and a quotation or short poem. Examine an example of this and it will demonstrate the harmony the artists were seeking and attaining.

The substance of the drawing is decided to a far greater degree than with western techniques by the material it is made on, the ink and the brushes. Supports have included fine silk and a large range of papers. The papers are often very soft and absorbent, thus they have to be given a treatment with alum to stop the drawing from running. Some of the papers are tinted and may have quite a rough and open texture. The brushes may be of wolf, goat, hare or badger hair and are set in bamboo handles with the head shaped to a point and without the characteristic bellying found with the sable and other brushes used in the West. The artist will tend to hold them nearly vertical, almost at a right angle to the surface of the paper and strokes are made with a decisive deliberation, the wrist should not rest on the paper as it could easily mar the surface. The ink will generally be met with ink sticks – these are small works of art themselves as they can bear quite elaborate decorations. The practice is to rub the ink stick into a little water on a special slab that will have a slightly roughened surface; from this several small pots of varying tonal strengths can be prepared. The whole practice of making the drawing is governed by traditional symbolism always with an inter-relationship between the drawing and calligraphy.

The art of oriental drawing goes back into antiquity; when tombs in the Hunan Province in China for the period 300 to 100 BC were excavated one of the earliest known writing brushes was found. The works of art are classified against the dynasties in China. The Han Dynasty, 206 BC to AD 221, is the base from which the foundations of pictorial expression can be traced, the history being highlighted by the great masters of particular subjects. Ch'ien Hsüan (c. 1235–1290), notable painter and calligrapher, the last of the four masters of flower and bird painting who set a fashion in the Five Dynasties and Northern Sung Period. Hsia Kuei (active 1180–1230), was noted for his highly individual sharp brushstrokes and the high degree of luminosity he could conjure just from ink alone. He had the skill also to give lively atmospheric effects. Shen Chou (1427–1509) was a leading exponent of ink drawing and calligraphy, he worked in the style of the Four Great Landscape Masters and founded a school in the Kiangsu Province. From this period also was T'ang Yin (1470–1523), one of the finest painters of the Ming Dynasty and one who became widely known in Europe. He had a talent for a delicate subtle treatment of figures, and his compositions were worked out with a carefully considered balance, but as with other leading masters, East or West, he has attracted numerous forgers. In the 17th century was Yün Shou-P'ing (1663–1690) who had an attractive lively brushwork when dealing with flowers and landscape, his pictures having a distinctive elegance.

Japanese brush drawing becomes most evident during the Kamakura period 1185–1333. There was the earlier master of landscape Kose No Kanaoko who was active during the latter part of the 9th century and who was considered to be the equal of Wu Tao-Tzu – the Chinese legendary figure who is credited with the start of figure painting and the use of silk as a support. In the 15th century was Sesshù (1420–1506), a celebrated painter with inks who followed the Chinese style; he rose above just the production of pastiche-like emulations. His brushwork was lively and he exercised considerable tonal control to evoke atmospheric effect. Maruyama Okyo (1733–1795) was a highly regarded realist painter of the Edo-Tokugawa period who founded a school that set out to follow the early Chinese artists, although latterly the main influence started to come from the West. There are three distinctive large types of Japanese painting: the Kakemono painted on a roll of silk or paper which is intended to be hung vertically; it would be mounted on rollers for storage: the Makemono, painted in a similar manner, but intended to be hung horizontally, and the Yamoto-E, a style of narrative painting on scrolls some of which were up to a hundred feet long – scroll painting was brought to Japan from China during the 8th century.

Pencil

Until about the early part of the 19th century the word pencil was applied exclusively to artists' brushes and, certainly during the first half of that century, there was occasional confusion with some publications. The pencil as we know it today is a comparatively recent introduction; the development being credited to Nicolas Jacques Conté in France and Joseph Hardmuth in Austria late in the 18th century. These instruments were the forerunners of today's sleek wood-cased pencils whose 'leads' are made of graphite and clay, with hardness varying from 9H down to the 6B which will give a delightfully soft, rich tone for drawing, although it will smudge quite easily and really should be fixed for permanence. Graphite was first mined in Barrowdale, England, in 1664 and at first used for writing with as small lumps mounted in sticks.

The origin of the term 'lead pencil' must be in the fact that the ancients used thin rods of lead to write with and possibly to sketch. Drawings made with pure lead on a suitable rough-toothed paper can be quite effective, although the lines will be a little weak, but if the drawing is exposed to the atmosphere, particularly if there is some industrial pollution, the lines will darken noticeably. Cennini talks of being able to draw on parchment that has not been treated with bone using a 'style' which was made of two parts lead and one part tin, well beaten with a hammer. He continues the advice saying that if a slip is made the mistake can be removed with crumbs of bread.

One of the masters of the pencil as a drawing instrument was Augustus Edwin John (1878–1961) born in Wales and trained at the Slade School. His pencil line drawings of figures and heads are models of sensitivity and economy of means; the anatomy often being suggested just by lines that changed in thickness to emphasise the limbs.

If tonal values are called for, they can be achieved by cross-hatching, as with pen and ink, or if the pencil used is of a soft degree the lines can be smudged with a finger-tip, a paper stump or a piece of rag. Pencil line drawings in conjunction with water-colour wash follow on the earlier custom of crayon with wash. If used with gouache, care is needed as the lines from soft grades can result in a 'pentimento', a ghosting through with some of the gouache colours. Examples of this can sometimes be seen in the work of Samuel Palmer. Papers are a matter of personal choice by the artist and can range from those used for pastel and charcoal to rag and cartridge, smooth or rough surface.

Pen and Ink

A drawing in any variation of this medium is a challenge; all the character and effect must be achieved by the artist with the line on the white or tinted paper and with the knowledge that correction is all but impossible. This need for perfection right away often is the stimulus that can push an artist to his best. Pen drawings by someone like Tiepolo or Rembrandt can be so vivid and full of life that it seems impossible such economy of means has been used.

It would be impossible to state exactly when the first pen was made, but certainly the early Egyptians used a form of pen cut from a reed to write on their sheets of papyrus. The Greeks and Romans had reed pens, the stylus and examples of bronze-nibbed pens have been discovered. The artists of the Far East cut pens from bamboos – a practice that is still continued.

The name pen is probably derived from the Latin *penna*, the English word as well as its equivalents in French with *plume* and German with *feder*, originally meant a wing-feather. One of the earliest specific allusions to the quill pen comes in the writings of St Isidore of Seville written in the early part of the 7th century; there are also words about the calamus or arundo, hollow tubular stalked grasses that grow in marshy lands.

Pen-and-ink drawings as separate entities did not really emerge until the Middle Ages; prior to this they had been a part of a written manuscript. These early drawings would have largely been done with quills, although the reed tradition carried right through. The most suitable feathers for quills were generally the pinions, those of the goose being the most favoured. In 1809 Joseph Bramah developed a machine for cutting up the quill into separate nibs; this was done by dividing the barrel into three and even four parts and cutting these transversely into lengths. In 1818 Charles Watt obtained a patent for gilding and preparing quills and pens. This was followed in 1822 when J. I. Hawkins and S. Mordan patented the making of nibs from horn and tortoiseshell, including the use of tiny diamonds, rubies or other very hard substances or the wrapping of a thin sheet of gold over the tip of the horn or tortoiseshell.

The first steel nib could have been made by a German, Johann Jannsen, in 1748 – the first in Britain being produced by a Birmingham split-ring manufacturer, Samuel Harrison, in 1780, apparently for a Dr Joseph Priestley. Early examples of steel nibs cum pens were being marketed in London about 1803; these were in the form of a thin barrel-like tube, the edges being brought together to form the slit and the sides being cut away. This gadget gave a stiff and unsatisfactory movement and sold for the then high price of five shillings. The real breakthrough came in 1822 when John Mitchell introduced machine-made steel pens; these were improved six years later by Josiah Mason who had been associated with the earlier Samuel Harrison. In 1831 Joseph Gillot elongated the points of the nibs, and it is to him that much credit can be given for the wide range of satisfactory drawing nibs that the artist can choose from. These small necessities for drawing received some elaborate treatments by the manufacturers to make them as perfect as possible. They were hardened and tempered, plunged in oil to anneal them; they were scoured in baths of dilute acid and polished in revolving cylinders, their points were ground with emery and in some cases coated with a special varnish of shellac. Experiments were made with other metals for the draughtsman, these included: gold, silver, zinc, German silver, aluminium and aluminium bronze.

The advantages of the steel pen nib are that it can be easily controlled and should hold the ink safely. An artist today will have a choice between a fine mapping-pen that will deliver a line as fine as spider's silk and nibs that can be as broad as an eighth of an inch. The inks that were used in the past have generally been made from lampblack plus assorted ingredients to improve colour, assist drying and adhesion. Whether it was the Chinese or the early Egyptians who first invented ink for drawing and writing is not clear, but they both must have thought up the idea about the same time, about 2500 BC. Sepia from the cuttlefish satisfied the Romans. The iron-gall ink prepared from an iron salt and tannin is mentioned in the 11th century by Theophilus. In the 16th century there were recipes in domestic encyclopaedias for preparing an ink from green vitriol, ferrous sulphate, with extracts from galls and different barks. The Chinese ink referred to today is similar to Indian ink, although it may have some extra ingredients to sharpen up the tone. Native Chinese inks and Japanese inks are still made in sticks which have to be rubbed down; there is also that rather fine Japanese ink Nerizumi, which has a subtle blue tinge and which will wash out into countless beautiful silvery tones. The manufacture of drawing ink in Japan has long traditions and the appreciation of the qualities amounts almost to a cult.

Besides the black inks, since the early Renaissance there have been many artists who have sought after satisfactory dark browns and warm sienna tints. Rembrandt had a great fondness for such inks, as can be noted with his numerous sketches. His method was often to combine the effects of the pen with brush washes using the same brown ink diluted with water and on a Japanese paper that had first been brushed over with a weak tone of the same brown; in another mood he might use the pen with the brown ink and then bring in areas of grey and black washes and some white heightening. Veronese was another attracted to the softer appearance of brown inks, using them for quick rough layouts with wash that could later be finalised into large paintings.

The Germans of the 16th century with their traditions of skills with engraving often tended to produce a drawing that had the somewhat stiff look of an engraving – although they could show great invention with details. There is a rather strange drawing with black ink by Hans Burgkmair dated somewhere between 1521 and 1523 entitled 'The Encounter between Valentin and Oursson in the Forest of Orleans'. Valentin was sent by his uncle King Pepin, into the forest of Orleans to apprehend the wild man who had plagued travellers. The drawing, measuring only about eight inches by eleven, shows the struggle in which Valentin was the victor. He led the wild man back to Paris where he was baptised Oursson. Later an interview with the magical Brazen Head in the Castle of the Lady Clerimond reveals that Valentin and Oursson were twin brothers, the sons of Empress Bellisant and Alexander of Greece. Oursson had been lost as an infant and brought up in the forest of Orleans by a bear. A German translation of the Carolingian story *Valentin and Orson* was first published in Basle in 1521. An interesting example how sometimes the background story round the subject of a drawing or a painting can increase the fascination. It can be noted how Burgkmair has drawn the sword of Valentin across the tree and cliffs, possibly a last-minute oversight.

Artists through the years have explored so many ways with pen and ink. Most inks have been waterproof, others have been purposely made non-waterproof so that they might be used on dampened paper to produce misty-edged lines. In the area of mixed media, pen and ink must have been combined with more media than any other. In the last hundred years or more the pen has been used with a rainbow selection of inks including white and even by some with metallic inks giving a gold or silver look. White and light-toned opaque inks have been effectively used on dark tinted papers.

Brush and Wash

The practice of this manner clearly originates with the technique of the East, although the European artists took it a long way from the stylistic manners of the Chinese and Japanese; they saw it as an extension of crayon drawing and used it with crayon, pen and ink and sometimes metal point drawings. The interesting difference between the European and Eastern approach is that although both schools use the brushes to produce definite stroke marks, the Chinese and Japanese work to a strict code of traditional symbolism whereas the European painter makes his brushes indicate in a broad manner the foliage, grasses, the details of figures – all of which are put in with a pleasing freedom yet end up very often with a well-balanced realism. The technique was at its height in the 16th and 17th centuries and then receded.

Silver Point

This last method to be described is arguably the most difficult and demanding for the artist. Like many other techniques the principle has been known for a long time, certainly the Romans knew about it as well as other metal points. There have been personal variations by artists, but basically the method has been something like this. A paper or parchment is prepared by having a thin coating applied to it of a substance that will provide a mild abrasive surface. This may be a white pigment, calcined bones have been and are favourites; Cennini talks of 'the thigh bone of a gelded lamb' as being suitable. With the calcined bone, some size from rabbit skins, pieces of parchment or hoof glue should be mixed, and the consistency aimed for should be similar to single cream. When this has hardened the artist carries out his drawing with a silver point that may have a round section or be flattened to increase the breadth of the strokes. The nasty part is that the silver point will make hardly a mark at all on plain paper and not much more impression on many of the grounded papers so that the artist cannot always know how the work is progressing. When he has finished the drawing is left exposed and what happens then is that the minute amounts of silver that have been abraded off by the calcined bone will tarnish and the very lovely warm brown lines will appear.

The grounds used have often been tinted with pale reds, greens, greys and blues which, combined with the line of a skilled master, can produce some of the most subtle and beautiful drawings of any media.

General Care of Drawings

What you should attempt yourself rests on how rare or valuable the example is. Certainly if it is of quality and there are signs of 'foxing' it should be left to the conservator. Recipes for bleaching may look harmless in print but even the mildest of them if mis-applied can wreak great damage on some of the drawing manners mentioned above. Leave tears and other damage to the professional. Although it may be safe to wash some pen and ink drawings, a drawing done with non-waterproof ink may start floating away before your eyes. With the pastels and chalks the risk is that they may not be fixed and rubbing in a corner to find out can leave a nasty mark.

The best advice if a worthwhile drawing has been purchased is to at least take advice before any recipe is tried on it. As mentioned earlier with other pictures, keep it under regular observation and if it has been mounted correctly and perhaps given a light spray at the back with a saturated solution of thymol in alcohol to ward off mould attack and does not evidence staining, which can generally be cleared by your conservator, it should give pleasure for a long time – a window into the world of an artist from yesterday.

Framing and Mounting

The picture frame that most feel is essential to complement a painting or drawing did not come into being until the early part of the 16th century. The origin can be traced back to the treatment of the doorway of a temple, palace or important building, where it was felt necessary to frame an impressive picture – either of the interior or looking out on to the exterior. Although in the earlier periods there are no signs of actual movable frames, there is plenty of evidence that enhancement of pictures or bas-reliefs was needed – in its most primitive form this would be a simple raised line to which later would be added elaborations at the corners of scrollwork, plant-forms and other motifs.

A number of the 16th-century frames for pictures show the influence of the doorway as they may have two upright columns topped by some form of classical entablature and use variations of carved mouldings. In panelled rooms numbers of pictures were set into panelling, sometimes with little more than small beaded mouldings, at other times more elaborate handling was included with swags of flowers, fruit or drapery. A legacy of the idea of having paintings set into the wall remains today with moulded rectangles, upright or horizontal, in wall panelling with no intention of placing pictures within them.

The creative surge of the Renaissance found yet another outlet with picture frames and there was a great profusion of beautiful examples produced and numbers of these still exist. Frames for pictures are usually square, oblong, round or oval with occasionally odd shapes to suit the whim of a patron or an artist. Basically frames have been made from wooden mouldings either carved, left plain or with composition decorations added. But there have been many cases where exotic and valuable materials have been incorporated; craftsmen have used ebony, ivory, bone, tortoiseshell, crystal, lapis lazuli, amber, mother-of-pearl, coloured lacquers, gold, silver and base metals and alloys, precious fabrics and at times rococo extravagances with

'Time smoking a picture' – an etching by William Hogarth.

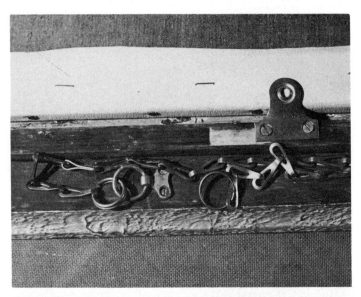

Top: *A brass 'shelf ear' being used to hold canvas into frame; also ring plate and picture chain.*

Bottom: *Painting knife with cranked handle can be used to clear obstructions.*

19th century fake by Franz Wolfgang Rohrich of a Lucas Cranach painting from the early 16TH century.

Modern forgery of an El Greco portrait . . .

with part of the top layer removed to show the picture underneath.

'The Annuciation', a genuine El Greco painting dating from c. 1586 now in the Toledo Museum of Art, Ohio, USA.

Two modern forgeries from Spain. Acrylic paint was used, and the paintings then damaged to give a false impression of age.

Detail from a 17th century Flemish painting on wood which was used as a fire screen, the picture has virtually disappeared.

The same after cleaning, before retouching by the author. A portrait of St Jerome now appears. The 17th century artist is de Craeyer.

'The rape of the Sabine women' by Luca Giordano (1632–1705).

Top left: As it arrived, after having been rolled in paper. It was buckled, cracked and torn, and the surface covered with thick coloured varnish.

Bottom left: After re-lining and during cleaning.

Above: After restoration complete.

Mould growth on a water colour and gouache. If neglected it would soon cover the whole of the painting.

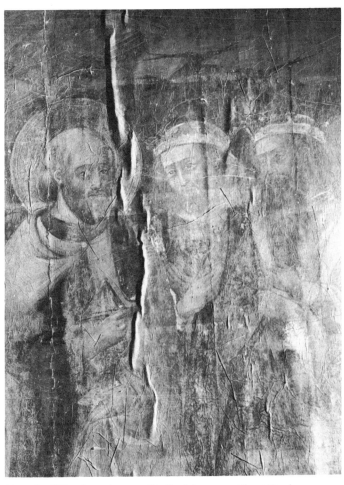

Example of blistering paint caused by flood damage and humidity change.

Top: Detail from a study of St Patrick painted in oils on copper during restoration to remove encrusted varnish.

Bottom: Shows craquelure of varnish containing bitumen.

'Chapeau de Paille' by Rubens during cleaning, showing areas of darkened varnish still to be removed.

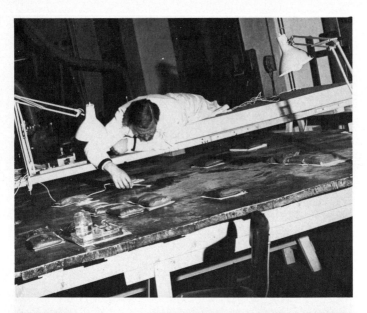

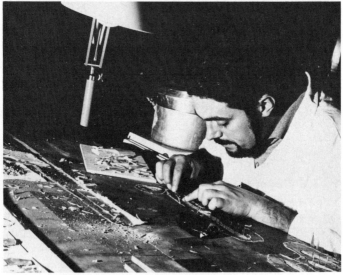

Work on paintings damaged in the Florence Flood of 1966.

Top: Treating blisters on an oil painting on wood.

Bottom: Building up damaged areas with balsa wood.

shells and strange materials. The carvers of the Renaissance and those down to the middle of the 18th century produced work of often outstanding elegance and style. In England the leading master was Grinling Gibbons (1648–1721) who was admired for his delicate carvings of fruit, flowers and birds; there was also Thomas Chippendale (1718–1779), although most of his often elaborate and rococo designs were intended for mirrors. In France frames of great taste were made and many could be counted among the most splendid and gorgeous objects of the gilded and artificial age. The introduction during the 17th century of larger sheets of glass gave the frame-making craft a considerable encouragement and this was further increased in the 18th century by the introduction of cheaper methods of making mirrors.

The last half of the 19th century in England saw a proliferation of fantasy with many of the frames intended for oil paintings. Composition moulding and casting made high decoration possible for a reasonable price and this drove some makers and patrons to extremes. Huge ornate gilded frames can still quite frequently be found; in many cases these are far too wide and gross for the unfortunate painting that cringes away in the middle. Often the decoration is cast and then stuck on to quite a plain channelled moulding. Time and rough handling can cause havoc with the composition which all too easily cracks and comes away in large chunks. Repairs, if desirable, are difficult and can be expensive. Towards the end of the century there was a fashion for the so-called 'Oxford' frames which were covered with rich fabrics or carved cork decoration. A ladies' magazine published in 1894 gave what was intended as a novel idea:

> An inexpensive picture frame may be made by covering a plain pine frame with varnish, then sprinkle it lavishly with either sand, oatmeal or rice. When thoroughly dry, cover the whole surface with gold paint.

Other materials were sometimes tried out for the main construction of the frames – at a stately home in the West Country vast frames for full-length portraits were found that were cast completely from a form of reinforced concrete.

Today there is a wide variety of frames to choose from and the selection will to a degree rest on how much can be afforded. There is no doubt that the right frame can considerably enhance most pictures, whereas the wrong one will spoil any possible enjoyment. Experience alone can teach what is just right and what should be the proportions of width of moulding for a particular picture size. Be careful when making a selection that the painting is not dwarfed by an overwide moulding or made to look unhappy with an overnarrow and meagre one. Broadly speaking, a twenty- by twenty-four-inch oil painting can take a moulding of around three inches wide, a forty- by fifty-inch picture can well compete with a five- or six-inch moulding.

There are three ways to approach framing: to buy wood mouldings and make up your own frames; to purchase mass-produced examples, or to go to a specialist frame-maker who will have the taste and experience to give your painting the best that it deserves.

If the choice is the first one, there are a few specialist tools that are required. These include some form of mitre-block or clamp, a tenon saw, a couple of 'G' cramps and at least one corner cramp. A smallish hammer, a supply of panel pins and adhesives, either synthetic or animal glue, will also be needed.

Wooden mouldings of various profiles can be found at most timber merchants or DIY shops. An even cheaper way can be to buy lengths of two- by one-inch timber and lengths of architrave mouldings, picture rail or glazing bars. With these can often be built up quite respectable mouldings from which the frame pieces can be cut.

The finishing of the frame will depend on the painting itself and also on the room in which it will hang. The timber may be left quite plain, the joints cleaned out with some fine sandpaper and then just given a very gentle finish with a beeswax polish. The wood can be painted over with emulsion colours or the frame may be given some form of texturing with a composition. The best material to use is *gesso*, which can be made up in a double saucepan with whiting and size; rabbit-skin glue or Scotch glue will also serve if they are diluted. The method is first to dissolve the size or glue in water and then to add enough whiting powder to achieve the texture of thick double cream. The *gesso* can then be applied to the frame by brushing on with a house painting brush, stippling the strokes can make for an attractive texture. Another way is after the *gesso* has been brushed on to use an old comb to give it a random look by criss-cross strokes or to comb it with a regular pattern. Once applied the *gesso* should be allowed about forty-eight hours to harden out. Next, with some medium coarse sandpaper, rub off any untoward pieces that are sticking up and also trim the corners.

If aiming for an 'antique' look, the general procedure runs as

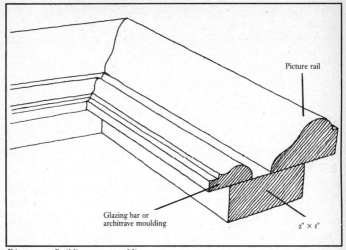

Diagram 4 Building up a moulding

Picture rail

Glazing bar or
architrave moulding

2″ × 1″

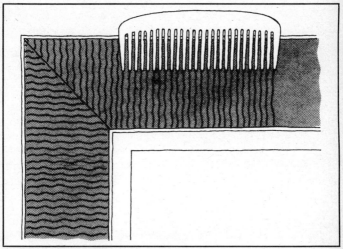

Diagram 5 Combing pattern into frame

follows. First isolate the *gesso* with either a thin coat of size or shellac dissolved to saturation point in methylated spirits. Let this dry and then brush on a layer of bole, a reddish brown, or burnt sienna with burnt umber will answer; the purpose of this is to provide an enriching foundation for the gilded effect. Gold leaf is expensive and is also tricky to lay, so fall back on one or other of the bronze powders. These may be purchased in several shades of gold, also silver, tin, pewter, bronze and copper; they may be mixed with special mediums or with acrylic medium. Additionally there are numerous gold paints and gold pastes in tubes and pots that can be bought. Apply whichever 'gold' finish has been chosen with a brush or piece of rag and when dry wipe on in a random fashion small areas of warm and cool oil colours diluted with white spirit; these are to provide a broken look for the next and final step. When the oil colours are dry, brush on an oatmeal or linen tinted distemper, and whilst this is still wet wipe back to expose some of the broken colours and the underlying gilding; when dry, just give a few finishing touches with a very small amount of a plain good quality furniture cream. This may all sound complicated but a little practice can produce interesting finishes that are tailored to the picture and its setting.

Having chosen the frame the painting must be fixed in place. All too often this is done with round or oval nails and some quite hefty clouts with a hammer. The concussion will not do the painting any good; often it can cause the mitred corners to separate and it will shake up any composition decoration. A very small outlay can provide a supply of either special spring clips or small metal plates that can be screwed on to the frame and will hold the painting quite securely. A picture twenty by twenty-four inches will need six fixers, two on each of the long sides and one on each of the shorter sides. If recourse is made to nails, keep them down to slender panel pins and use as little hammering as possible. Never, never drive them through the stretcher and then into the frame; if this is done it is nearly impossible to remove them without damage to the stretcher, possibly the canvas and the frame.

The hanging cord, wire or chain should be attached to the frame by adequate screw-eyes or small metal plates with a ring. If picture chains are used, split rings will be necessary to attach them to the screw-eye or ring and the picture hook. Unglazed paintings are best hung with a slight cant forward as this will to a large degree prevent dust falling on to the surface of the paint-ings – place the screw-eyes or metal plates a third of the way down from the top. This method will serve with glazed pictures as well; the slight lean forward will make them easier to see as the glass is less likely to catch reflections.

All too often paintings purchased at sales have their frames quite badly damaged. Serviceable repairs are possible with patience. Proprietory modelling pastes can be used or the *gesso*

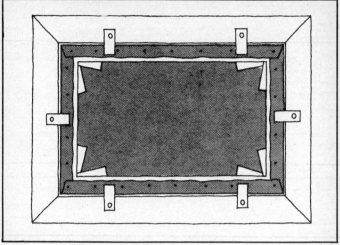

Diagram 6 Fixing canvas in frame with metal strips and screws

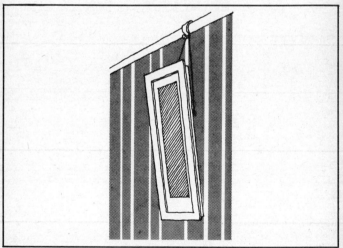

Diagram 7 Position screw eye ⅓ from top of frame

mentioned above. Small cracks can be filled by pressing the paste in with a finger tip. Larger areas should first have two or three small dressmaker's pins pushed in around the wood, these will help key the paste and hold it securely. Once the paste mends are dry they can be treated with a gold paint or gold paste. If the repairs 'stare' too much when dry, brush them over with raw umber or burnt umber diluted with white spirit.

Sometimes a painting bought at auction will be found to be slightly too small for the frame and this means there will be unsightly gaps round the edge. This is quite simple to remedy by fitting a fillet inside the rabbet and projecting from it; this can materially increase the width of the frame by up to about an inch and will greatly improve the overall look. The fillet can be a plain wood strip that, after cutting to shape and fitting, may be painted a soft neutral warm grey to harmonise with the painting and the frame. A more satisfactory fillet can be made by using either strips of thick cardboard or wood and covering them with a good linen canvas. When doing this, be careful not to use too much adhesive, for if it comes through the canvas it will cause staining. Be careful also to cut the ends of the strips to fit as snugly as possible and at an angle of forty-five degrees; they should be stuck into position behind the rabbet not tacked or nailed.

The frames for water colours, gouaches, pastels and other drawings in general should have a narrower moulding than for an oil. If a drawing is placed in a great heavy frame it will be overshadowed. Depending on the size of the drawing, mouldings between one inch and one and three-quarters of an inch should prove suitable. As with frames for oils, mouldings can be bought and then made up yourself or there will be a large choice from specialist frame-makers. Some art dealers may have available kits of ready-cut frame mouldings that may be quite simply assembled with clips or screws.

The putting together of the narrower mouldings can prove more difficult than the heavier variety. When driving in the panel pins at the corners either have the moulding held in a cramp or have it supported by a heavy weight. The wood mouldings may be left plain or may be painted with emulsion colours; they may also be treated with *gesso*, as with the oil frames. If the mouldings are oak they can be treated with wax polish or have whiting rubbed into the grain, which can give a pleasant appearance.

In many ways more important than the frame is the mount. The vital point with this is to arrive at a satisfactory proportion for the 'window' in relation to the width of the mount, the size of the picture and the moulding. If in doubt, examine some of the drawings and their mounts in galleries. This proportion of the window must be correct otherwise the whole effect will be spoilt. One basic rule is that the width of the mount from the top and the two sides of the frame should be the same and the width from the bottom of the frame should be slightly more.

Mounting cards come in various thicknesses and may also be tinted or covered with tinted papers; puchase as good a quality as possible as the cheaper types which are thin will only look 'mean' when in the frame.

The 'window' should be cut out with a really sharp knife running along a steel rule and held at about an angle of forty-five degrees. It is best to cut the mount with the card resting on several thicknesses of paper as this will allow the blade of the knife to come right through and thus ensure that essential clean cut to the sides of the mount.

Some prefer the so-termed 'French' mounts – those that have decorative lines and bands round the window. They may consist of plain double lines or thin bands of colour or combinations of these and gold. Care should be taken that the colours used complement rather than overwhelm the picture. Lines are best put in with an architect's ruling pen and may be of black, slightly watered-down, or sepia. Painting in the coloured bands will need a very steady hand and is probably best done with a flat, soft-hair brush. If using a combination of lines and bands, paint in the bands first and then put in the lines, as doing it this way makes for a much neater finish. Another finish which will suit particular pictures is to paint just the bevelled cut round the window with gold or silver. When doing this it is best to work from the back of the mount.

Another treatment for the mount can be to face it with a textile – such as linen or velvet – depending on the drawing. To do this, first of all apply an adhesive to the whole of the face of the mount, then when it is tacky gently press the selected textile into place. Leave to set for several hours and then make a cross cut diagonally between the corners; fold back each side and stick down to the back of the mount and trim off any surplus.

When fixing the drawing to the mount, never stick it firmly all the way round. It may be fixed with four narrow strips of white paper which should be of less strength than the paper of the drawing. The strips of paper, or 'guards' as they are called, should reach for about three-quarters of the way along each side and certainly be as long as the side of the window. Use a good quality water-soluble mounting paste, not a synthetic one, and, nor is rubber cement really to be recommended. If the drawing is slightly buckled or has some fold marks it is normally safe to slightly dampen the back with a small sponge or piece of cotton wool that has been dipped in water and well wrung out; do this before fixing into position with the 'guards'. Depending on the thickness of the paper that carries the drawing the picture may be mounted with a single 'guard' at the top. Never dry mount a drawing because this can be difficult to reverse.

The Victorians, and those coming after them, sometimes had a grievous habit of mounting a drawing so that it was stuck down all over and completely on to a thick brown straw-board. First this is very likely to cause staining, secondly it can encourage mildew and lastly it is very tricky to get off again, particularly if the picture is in pastel, charcoal or gouache. If the drawing is not greatly valued an attempt can be made by soaking the mount in luke-warm water. Normally after about an hour it should start to release the picture which should then be laid face down on clean blotting-paper on a flat smooth surface such as glass, and the back of the drawing should then be gently scraped with a plastic palette knife to remove the often liberal amounts of Scotch or fish glue.

To complete the task, lay the frame and glass face down on a stout table or bench that is covered with a soft cloth or old blanket. Lower the mount and drawing into position and then the backing board. This last should always be of hardboard, never three-ply as the woodworm family absolutely adore the latter. When tacking the backing board into place, always support with a heavy weight the part of the moulding that is being tacked in order to absorb the hammer blows. Seal the backing to the moulding with an adhesive tape and place the hanging screw-eyes about one third of the way down.

A precaution against mildew and 'foxing' can be to place a piece of impregnated paper between the drawing and the backing board. The paper can be treated with a spray of a saturated solution of thymol in alcohol.

One other problem may face the collector, and that is with a map that can have relevant printing on the reverse side that needs to be visible, or a page from an artist's sketch-book with drawings on both sides. A moulding should be selected with a deep rabbet which will take the thickness of two sheets of glass and mounts and, if possible, fit these four exactly. The procedure is to cut two mounts the same size with identical windows, mount the drawing between them and place with the two sheets of glass into the rabbet of the frame. To finish, what is needed are some strips of wood similar in nature to the frame. Fix these into position with small panel pins, not an adhesive.

Picture lights are often effective, especially in a rather dark room. Choose with care and keep the wattage as low as possible in line with good visibility. It is probably best to have the lights fixed at the top of the frame rather than the bottom as then any heat generated will dissipate into the air above the picture. The types of light available include the strip bulbs, also spots with reflective backs to the bulbs and fittings that have reflectors in them. Shuttered spot lights may also be procured but experiment with these to be sure that they will suit the particular case; they can be effective but they may also give a false appearance and make the painting resemble a colour transparency.

Lastly, a thought on travel for the pictures; they are prone to damage but if a few simple precautions are taken, journeys can be made in safety. Glazed pictures should have a criss-cross of sticky tape. Oils in heavy frames should have the corners protected with rolls of corrugated paper bent round them and stuck on to the back of the frame. Wherever possible, pack the pictures vertically with a piece of stout card or hardboard in between each. Take care that the pictures are packed in the car or vehicle so that they are firmly in place and cannot suddenly shift.

Pictures can often be the most valuable part of the contents of a house, treat them all as though they are very fragile – ten patient minutes with handling can quite often avert damage.

Glossary of terms concerned with Pictures

Abozzo
The first sketch or underpainting for an oil; the French use the term *frotte,* also called 'dead colouring', from the habit of using monochrome at this stage.

Academy Board
A cheap support for oil painting, a type of pasteboard about 3 mm (⅛ inch) thick which is sized and then primed with white lead. Introduced during the 19th century it is now almost obsolete, being replaced by oil painting paper and other proprietary boards.

Achromatic Colours
White, black and grey.

Advancing colours
Warm strong tints such as red and orange which tend to give the impression of coming forward. The cool colours such as blues and violets tend to recede.

Alla Prima
Literally to paint a picture in one sitting, applies most to oils, The French use the term *au premier coup.*

Analogous Colours
Those that are very close to each other in the colour circle and may easily be mistaken – orange and red, sea green and blue etc.

Aquarelle
Another name for pure water colour.

Aureole
The celestial crown, a halo, the radiance surrounding the head of a holy figure in medieval and Renaissance art.

Aureole

Baroque
The dominant style in Europe particularly on the Continent during the 17th century. It was dynamic and tended to be theatrical, using realism, illusion-

ism and ornate forms to achieve its effects. It should not be confused with rococo, the style which followed it. With baroque the artists were revelling in a new-found mastery of design and composition.

Bell's Medium
19th-century oil painting medium prepared from blown linseed oil with oil of spike; largely superseded by other mediums.

Bleeding
The action of one colour running into another. It is most applicable to water colour and when used intentionally can produce some exciting and often beautiful effects.

Bright
A type of brush preferred by some for oil painting, it is named after the Englishman who invented it. The brush may have bristles or sable hair, the length of the tip is one and a half times its width.

Bristol Board
Stiff durable ply-produced cardboard suitable for water colour or gouache also pen and ink work.

Broken Colour
A term first associated with the French Impressionists in the 19th century. It infers the optical mixing as seen when on the support rather than the physical mixing on the palette. The colours are put down with small strokes close to one another.

Burnisher
An instrument to bring a high polish to a metal surface such as gold, silver or other leaf in a painting. It is either shaped from hardened steel or the semi-precious stone agate. The 15th-century artist-writer Cennini suggested using a dog's tooth or a piece of hematite.

Cabinet Picture
Somewhat obsolete term for small easel paintings.

Camel Hair
'Camel hair brushes' is a general term for cheap varieties; the hair used is not camel but comes from the squirrel.

Camera Lucida
An optical device which, by the use of a prism, makes it possible to copy an object. The rays of light from the model are reflected by the prism and produce an image on the canvas or paper. By adjusting the prism and inserting magnifying lenses the size of reproduction can be made smaller or larger. It was invented by Richard Hooke in 1674, but was not widely used until 1807, when it was redesigned and patented by Wilson Hyde Wollaston.

Canvas Board
Heavy cardboard with cotton or linen canvas glued to one side with the edges folded over to the back. The face is primed in the same manner as an Academy board.

Canvas Sizes
Standard sizes in England and America are: (in inches)

Bishop's whole length	70×106
Whole length	58×94
Small whole length	52×88
Bishop's half length	44×56
Half length	40×50
Small half length	34×44

| Kit-cat | 28×36 |
| Three-quarter | 25×30 |

The Kit-cat size was named after the 18th-century London club kept by Christopher Cat, whose members were painted by Sir Godfrey Kneller all to the same size.

Carnation

A period term used with portrait painting especially for delicate tints with a lady's face.

Cartoon

Full-size drawing prepared as a guide for mural or easel paintings.

Cartridge Paper

Cheap white drawing paper made from wood or vegetable pulp. The name derives from the time when strong cheap paper was used in the manufacture of cartridges.

Cauteria

Collective term for the equipment needed for the applying of colours during encaustic painting.

Chiaroscuro

The handling of light and shade. Many painters in the past have been fascinated by the effects of light, its direction, reflected lights and what goes on in the shadows. Masters of this art are Rembrandt, Caravaggio, de La Tour and Wright of Derby.

Chromatic Colours

All those except black, grey and white.

Complementary Colours

A pair of colours usually considered to be in contrast to one another, thus on opposite sides of the colour circle – green and red, blue and orange, yellow and violet.

Conversation Piece

A painting which incorporates two or more portraits of people, sitting or standing naturally in a room as if they were at home, or outside in a garden or rural setting. Popular during the 18th century and often produced by Arthur Devis and Johann Zoffany.

Craquelure

Hair-line cracks that appear on an oil, they may be in the paint or varnish.

Degraded Colours

Those that have been mixed with greying tints and so have their normal brilliance or truth brought down. Also the over-mixing of colours that tends to give them a dull, muddy appearance, applies mostly to oils and acrylics.

Driers

Substances that are added to oil paints to hasten the drying. The idea is, if possible, to make all the colours dry at an even speed. Quick-drying pigments include umbers, siennas, ochres and flake white.

Ear-Wax

An occasional additive to some lake colours to improve their flow, an idea of the late 17th century.

Ébauche

The first lean underpainting with oils.

Écorché Figure

An anatomical figure of a man or an animal that is shown without its skin so that muscle arrangements can be studied. Andrea Vesalius (1514-1564), the Flemish anatomist, was one who left some remarkable drawings in this vein. His chief work was *De Corporis Humani Fabrica*, 1543.

Eidograph
An instrument similar to a pantograph which an artist may use to reduce or enlarge his drawings.

Epigone
Imitator or follower of a great artist to whom he is inferior.

Face-painting
The old term for portrait-painting, hence the practiser of the art was simply termed a face-painter by writers of the 16th and 17th centuries.

Figurative Painting
A term to describe realist or naturalist painting as opposed to abstract painting.

Filler
Inert pigments which have no tinting power of their own that are mixed to add bulk to more expensive colours. Kaolin is one of the most used substances.

Film
In painting it is a continuous layer of paint. A dried out paint layer is referred to as a paint film when talking about behaviour, composition and structure.

Finger Painting
A technique which originated in China. With this the finger is dipped into the colour and used in the manner of a brush. In one method the paper is first made wet and next spots of colour are placed on the surface and then manipulated with the fingers to make pictures. As quite thick water colour or gouache may be used additional gum or size is added to aid permanence.

Fitch
A brush made from the fur of a polecat. It is also a brush made in a chisel shape with the ferrule tapering towards the handle, either bristle or hair.

Fixative
A liquid, which may be shellac in alcohol or synthetic cellulose solution, that is intended to be sprayed as a fine mist on to charcoal, soft pencil, chalk, some crayons or pastel to consolidate the drawings. The spraying must be done with care because too heavy an application can flood and float the drawing away. Tests should always be made with pastel as the fixative can alter tone and tint values.

Floating Signature
One that is put on top of the varnish. If found it is very often the signal that either the signature and/or the painting is fraudulent. It is very unlikely a painter of a particular picture would sign on top of the varnish, it would almost always be on the actual paint. A raking light can sometimes help in picking up such a device.

Fluorescence
The characteristics whereby certain substances become luminous or seem to emit light when viewed during an examination with ultra-violet light.

Fore-edge Painting
A strange vagary of the artist. It means the painting of a picture on the edges of the pages in a book. To do this the artist fanned out the pages, painted his picture and then the book was squared up once more and its edges gilded in

the usual manner with expensive or special editions. The trick was that the picture was invisible in the normal way until the pages were once more fanned out.

Foreshortening
The technique, particularly with figures, of giving the impression that a particular part is turned towards the viewer.

Frottage
The process of making rubbings of the impressions of objects and textures on quite soft papers. Max Ernst (1891–1976) was one Surrealist who explored the idea (see page III).

Frottis
French term for a thin glaze or wash of colour; may also be applied to a thin scumble or the traces of oil colour when it has been partially wiped away.

Fugitive Colours
Pigments which are liable to fade when exposed to bright light; that may alter when mixed one with another; colours that may darken, crack or produce other disfigurements with time. Many paintings of the late 18th and the 19th centuries were ruined because bitumen was included.

Gallery Copy
A copy made from a famous picture. If these were made in the better known galleries the back of the canvas of the copy was indelibly stamped by the authorities to prevent it being fraudulently sold.

Gallery Varnish or Tone
A dark copal or tinted varnish that was applied by curators and dealers in pictures in the 19th century to answer the demand for a fashion for this type of finish. John Constable was one of those who had his paintings temporarily disfigured by this treatment.

Gallipot
Small porcelain or glazed earthenware container used by painters to hold their oils and mediums.

Garzone
Italian for an artist's apprentice or studio boy.

Genre Painting
A loose term to describe simple representation of everyday life without imaginative or romantic treatment. The manner more or less started with the Dutch painters of the 16th and 17th centuries; men like De Hooch, Metsu and Steen. It had a considerable popularity in England during the 19th century but in a somewhat debased form, being over-sentimentalised.

Giornata
Italian, literally the 'day piece' or 'day's work' for the painter when working in fresco.

Golden Section (also Golden Mean)
A rule of proportion known from earliest Classical times. It lays down a relationship of a line or figure to the whole of the picture. It was originally worked out by Vitruvius and in plain geometrical terms lays down the division of a straight line into two parts so that the proportion of the smaller part to the greater is the same as the greater part to the whole. Many artists have employed the golden

section in the composition of their pictures; but broadly speaking composition is an intuitive art rather than one that has to infallibly follow a set rule.

Grisaille

Monochrome painting which is carried out in tones of grey. It was often used in the imitation of bas-relief and as such is especially suited to architectural subjects. It was also used as an underpainting by the Northern Renaissance artists, thus some extant grisaille paintings are actually unfinished pictures. Excellent examples are St John the Baptist and St John the Evangelist which are on the backs of the two folding sections of the 'Adoration of the Lamb' by the Van Eyck brothers in St Bavos in Ghent.

Grotesque

A term applied to a decorative ornament which might be painted or carved. The ornament consisted of imaginative and fantastic human and animal figures and mystical objects, foliage and flowers interlaced in a fantasy of shape and colour. It is often found in Greek and Roman palaces and the manner had a revival in Italy during the 15th century.

Ground

The name that is applied to the coating of the surface or support on which the painting is to be made; thus gesso can be the ground on a wooden panel, sizing and priming is the ground on canvas.

Half-tone

One that lies between white and black, bright and dark.

Hard Edge

A painting manner in which the component parts of the composition are crisply defined, presenting a somewhat austere effect. A number of painters have chosen this manner; it is more often geometric than representational.

Hatching

Shading or modelling with fine, closely set lines – if a second set of lines goes over the first at an angle it is called cross-hatching. The method was and is often used with egg tempera.

Hiding Power

The opacity of a pigment; it describes its ability to cover underpainting and construction lines or sketches.

High Renaissance

The period in Italy round about 1500 when the ideals of the period bloomed to the full. It embraces the work of Leonardo da Vinci, Michelangelo, Raphael and others; it was the height of perfection of this wonderful artistic upsurge.

Hogarth's Line

A supposed line of beauty, a term introduced by William Hogarth (1697–1764) in his book The Analysis of Beauty (1753). It consists of a graceful double curve which Hogarth felt to be the basis of all successful design.

Illusionism

The technique of creating as closely as possible an illusion of visual reality. Every device, such as foreshortening, perspective etc., is used. The French name for this type of work is *trompe l'oeil*. It is often carried out in tempera as greater detail can be obtained than with oil. Illusionist works were in fashion during the Hellenistic period and were also popular with the Romans; signs of it occur with the Pompeian murals, such as those in the House of the Vetii. During the Renaissance architects commissioned it to extend the appearance of their interiors. There is the simulated apse in the Church of St Satiro, Milan, designed by Donato Bramante in 1514. The perspective murals of the Presenti Brothers carried out about 1580 in such places as the Palazzo de Giardino, Sabbinioneta, Mantua, challenge the eye to see where the illusion begins and ends.

Impressionism

One of the most revolutionary movements in the history of painting. In the 19th century painters, particularly in France, freed themselves of academic rulings and found a new realism. Light was of the primary concern, its effects on colours, on the whole scene in front of them. Then came the putting down of the paint; they broke with the old traditions of over-lapping and lapping strokes and exchanged these for staccato dabs, so that the areas of colour were broken; generally they worked with a bright palette that contained roughly the colours of the spectrum with no earth colours. The three leaders of this demonstration towards freedom were: Claude Monet (1840–1926), Camille Pissarro (1830–1903) and Alfred Sisley (1840–1899).

The name Impressionism was coined by a derisive critic reporting on an exhibition of their work in Paris in 1874; Monet's *'Impression: Soleil levant'* gave the hack his chance. The roots of the ideas they exploited came from painters such as Constable and Turner, also Hogarth, and as far back as Frans Hals with his virtuosity of brushwork.

Key

The general effect of colour and light. Predominance of light colours would be high-key, of dark colours low-key. It may also be applied to the roughness or texture of a paper intended for pastel, chalk or charcoal.

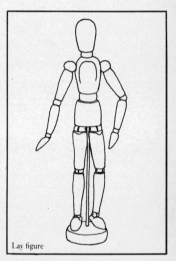
Lay figure

Lay Figure

Jointed wooden figure, either quite small or up to life-size, that may be used as a substitute for the sitter. The figure is so constructed that the limbs can only be moved in the same way as an actual human figure. Popular 18th-century portrait-painters' used them dressed in the clothes the sitter demanded and thus saved the clients many arduous hours sitting still.

Levigation
The grinding of pigments in a wet state.

Liber Studiorum
A collection of etched or mezzotint prints either made or designed by Joseph Mallord William Turner (1775–1851); it was brought out by him between 1807 and 1819 with the intention that it should act as a guide to landscape. Claude Lorrain (1600–1682) made a similar folio of the paintings he had already sold, this was called 'Liber Veritatis'.

Licence
The term 'artist's licence' actually means selection. When a painter looks at a subject he will choose those parts of it which he feels are necessary to portray the scene or sitter as he sees them.

Limning
Obsolete term for drawing or painting.

Medium
It can be the technique chosen by the painters: oils, water colour, egg tempera, pastel, charcoal, pen and ink, silver point etc., or it can be the liquid that is added to a colour to increase its fluidity.

Megilp (also McGuilp, magilp)
An 18th-century oil painting medium, a mixture of linseed oil, mastic varnish and lead driers; it had a jelly-like consistency, slightly cloudy and yellow. It did make colours easy to work but it could leave a brittle paint-film and cause heavy cracking. Chemists as early as 1826 warned against its use.

Metal Supports
Copper sheets have been used primarily, although some works have been carried out on aluminium, iron, steel and zinc. The only medium for the early painters that could be used was oils; today acrylics can be used. The metal sheets have to be carefully degreased and then given some form of grounding, they may also be slightly roughened. Paintings on metal sheets are susceptible to damage by temperature change and, if the sheets are thin, by careless handling.

Monotype
A method that lies between painting and printing. The artist can paint his picture on a hard surface such as glass and then, while the paint is still wet, press a sheet of paper down onto it and take a print which will have the freedom of a painting.

Neutral Colour
One that has no definite hue, such as grey.

Nuance
A very subtle and delicate variation in tone, colour or light in painting. An almost imperceptible difference, often only seen by the trained eye.

Oleograph
A picture that is printed in oil-colour inks to imitate an oil painting.

Palette
This may either be the wooden,

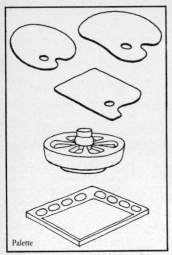

Palette

ceramic or enamelled metal surface on which the painter mixes his colours, or the selection of colours that he works from.

Palimpsest

Literally meaning 'scraped again'. A parchment on which the writing or illumination has been erased; this can be done by abrasion, washing or bleaching and thus the parchment can be used again. In modern usage the term has come to mean any canvas, panel or paper that has been reused.

Panorama

A landscape that could be painted along a wall or walls or on a long roll of canvas or paper. It was an 18th- and 19th-century display exhibition technique which was popular for its educational and entertainment value. The longest one and probably the largest picture ever painted was a panorama painted by John Banvard (1815–1891) in 1846. It showed the Mississippi for 1200 miles and was itself about 5000 feet long and 12 feet high; an overall area of 1.3 acres. It is thought that it was destroyed by fire.

Pantograph

An instrument similar to an eidograph, for reducing or enlarging designs or sketches, it worked by a system of levers.

Paper

A substance made from wood-pulp, other vegetable matter, rags or other materials with fibres. It is thought that the first papers were made in China about 105 AD. The invention then was probably carried from the Far East by the Turks during the Dark Ages. The first appearance in Europe seems to have been during the 12th

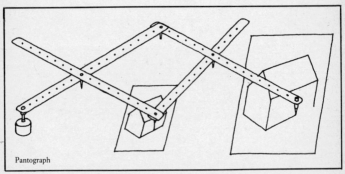

Pantograph

century. Rag papers, generally chosen for water colour, are made in three surfaces: 'Hot Pressed', with a smooth shiny surface; 'Not' with a matt surface and 'Rough' which can be very coarse grained and heavy. There are also tinted papers available for the artist and specialist ones for pastel, charcoal, chalk and pencil drawing. A number of the papers bear the name of artists such as Turner, Cox, de Wint.

Papyrus
Writing and painting material made by the early Egyptians that was something like paper. It was made from the reed *Cyperus papyrus;* strips of the reed were laid over each other, then they were soaked with water and pounded, and finally dried in the sun.

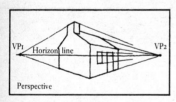

Perspective

Perspective
A geometric solution for producing the impression of the third dimension in a picture. For the artist's work externally, one or two vanishing points may be used; for interior work normally only one. Other forms of perspective include worm's eye view looking up and bird's eye view looking down.

Pettenkofer's Process
A method of revivifying the varnish film on an old oil painting. The picture to be treated would be placed in a special air-tight box on some kind of support so that it was face down. Flat containers of alcohol or ether were slipped in underneath and the fumes from these gave a temporary span of life to the old varnish. It could be a risky one for the painting and is now seldom used. Max von Pettenkofer was the inventor towards the end of the last century.

Pictograph
A record that is made up of pictorial symbols as opposed to letters.

Pinxit, Pictor
A term often added to the name or initials of an artist on a painting, or a copy of an original. Literal meaning is to indicate that the one signing the picture had painted it or copied it.

Plein Air
An expression in vogue during the latter part of the 19th century to state that a painting was carried out in the open air, out-of-doors.

Pochade
A rapid rough sketch of a landscape executed out-of-doors from nature; generally it would be the intention of the artist to use the *pochade* as a guide for working up a larger more finished picture.

Polyptych
A set of paintings on hinged panels, more than three, but generally five.

Port-crayon
Metal or bamboo holder for pieces of pastel, chalk or charcoal.

Primary Colours

Red, yellow and blue; the secondary colours are orange, green and violet.

Profil Perdu

Translated literally means 'lost profile'. The method of posing a figure so that the head is partially turned away and only the contour of the cheek, chin and throat are seen. In the early days of portrait painting this type of posing would never have been used; it became popular with the work of the Impressionists and many artists of this century.

Quadratura

An illlusionist method of painting on ceilings and walls to give them the impression of great space with imaginative treatment of the figures and details.

Quivering Brush

Chinese painting techniques; it is used to give the impression of the movement of waves and is applied with the brush held vertically using literally 'quivering' or vibrating strokes.

Raindrop Stroke

Technique for shading in Chinese painting. It was developed by the southern school of the T'ang Dynasty and is carried out by using small pointed oval strokes.

Rebus

A heraldic term for a pictorial design which suggests the owner's name. In the picture 'The Ambassadors' the German artist Hans Holbein (1494–1543) used a strange diagonally distorted skull as a form of rebus, it stretches across the foreground of the picture.

Rendering

A rendered drawing is one that is treated with repeated washes of one or just a few colours to build up the effect.

Retouching Varnish

A light varnish which can be used very soon after a painting is completed, or during the painting of the picture if certain parts have gone 'dead'. It is so thin that it will not cause cracking.

Rococo

An escapist style of decoration and approach to painting that flourished in the mid-18th century. Lavish use of motifs and embellishments characterised the manner.

Royal Academy

The British Royal Academy was founded in 1768. In 1760 London had no public galleries of art; it was the energy of such as Hayman, supported by the Society of Arts (founded in 1754) that supplied this long felt need by arranging an exhibition. In 1761 a second one was organised with works by, among others, Hogarth, Gainsborough and Reynolds. These were the first steps. In November 1768 Sir William Chambers, backed up by twenty-two artists, put forward the idea to George III and the King signed the Instrument for the Foundation of the Royal Academy on 10 December 1768. The first President was Sir Joshua Reynolds.

Sand Painting

An odd form of pictorial expression which was first practised by the North American Indians, notably the Navaho tribe. The pictures were sometimes twenty feet across and were executed on the floor, various coloured sands being sprinkled to build up symbolic patterns; the pictures were often used in religious and magic rites.

Sfumato

Evolved from the word in Italian for 'smoked', it is a method of achieving subtle graduation of tone from dark to light often with hazy outlines. Leonardo was one who used it most effectively.

Sgraffito

Scratching or cutting through a layer of colour to expose an underlying second, third or more colour, or to expose the ground. The term was introduced in 1907 by Otto von Falke although such treatment had been used in different ways for a long time.

Siccatives

Substances that can be added to speed up the drying time of oil colours.

Singeries

Paintings which showed monkeys dressed and behaving as people. Watteau was one who produced some examples.

Sotto in Su

Extreme foreshortening to give an effect of floating figures in ceiling work, the overall appearance is one of romantic and imaginative fantasy. Giovanni Battista Tiepolo (1696–1770) was a master of the technique.

Tortillon

A paper stump made from rolled-up blotting paper for manipulating pastel, chalk or charcoal drawings.

Trompe L'oeil

(see Illusionism)

Ultramarine Ash

By-product of the refining of natural ultramarine; it consists of a remnant of lapis lazuli with greyish rock; it can be used as a pigment but the colour is low in tinting power and rather dull.

Vehicle

In painting this refers to the liquid in which a pigment is ground or suspended.

Velatura

A mode of glazing adopted by some of the earlier Italian painters, with this the colour was rubbed on with the fingers or the flattened palm of the hand.

Vignette

A picture, landscape or portrait or other subject which has the edges blended, graded or softened away.

Wetting Agent

A liquid added in small amounts to water colour to reduce the surface tension and thus increase the flow of the colours. Ox gall has been the traditional one, but now synthetic substances close to detergents are being introduced.

Index

Acknowledgement is due to the following for permission to reproduce certain photographs in this book:
Abbot Hall Art Gallery, Kendal xiii (top)
Bristol City Art Gallery, xlii, xliii
British Museum, London, xxxiii
Christie's Fine Art Ltd., i, ii (top), iii, iv (top), v, vi, vii, viii (bottom), ix, x (top), xiv, xix (bottom), xxii (bottom), xxiii, xxiv, xxv, xxvi, xxvii
Doerner Institute, Munich, xxxv, xxxvi, xxxvii
Fischer Fine Arts Ltd., xvi
French Government Tourist Office, xvii (top)
Marlborough Fine Art Ltd., xv (bottom)
Paul Mitchell, ii (bottom), iv (bottom)
National Gallery, London, xlvii
Orbis Publishing Ltd., xxxii
Sotheby Parke Bernet, viii (top), x (bottom), xi, xviii, xix (top), xx, xxii (top), xxviii, xxix, xxx, xxxi
Tate Gallery, London, xiii (bottom), xv (top)
Toledo Museum of Art, Ohio, xxxviii
Victoria & Albert Museum, London, xxi
Victor Waddington, xii
Dean and Chapter of Winchester Cathedral, xvii (bottom)
The remaining photographs are the author's copyright.